D0374913

Candles in the Dark

The Authorized Biography of

FR. RICHARD HO LUNG

AND THE MISSIONARIES OF THE POOR

Candles in the Dark

The Authorized Biography of

FR. RICHARD HO LUNG

AND THE MISSIONARIES OF THE POOR

JOSEPH PEARCE

SAINT BENEDICT✝PRESS
Charlotte, North Carolina

Cover design by Chris Pelicano

Cataloging-in-Publication data on file with the Library of Congress.

ISBN: 978-1-61890-398-3

Published in the United States by
Saint Benedict Press, LLC
P.O. Box 410487
Charlotte, NC 28241
www.saintbenedictpress.com

Printed and bound in the United States of America.

For Bob and Conor Gallagher,
In Deepest Gratitude

CONTENTS

Prologue

....

THE ACCEPTANCE
OF SUFFERING

One has to accept sorrow for it to be of any heal-
ing power, and that is the most difficult thing in
the world. . . . A priest once said to me, "When you
understand what accepted sorrow means, you will
understand everything. It is the secret of life."
—Maurice Baring, *Darby and Joan*

FATHER Richard Ho Lung, founder of the Missionaries of
the Poor, one of the fastest growing religious congregations in the world, is a great lover of literature, as he is a great
lover of a great many things. In his earlier life, prior to giving
up the creature comforts to offer himself in free service to the
poor, he taught literature at university and high school level. He
is particularly fond of the writing of T. S. Eliot, Gerard Manley
Hopkins, and Fyodor Dostoyevsky. I have no idea whether
Father Ho Lung has ever read Maurice Baring's last novel, from
which the above quote is plucked. I have no doubt, however,
that he would agree with the words spoken by Baring's fictional
priest. The acceptance of sorrow or suffering is the secret of life.
When we understand that we will understand everything, or, if

not everything, we will at least understand everything necessary to save us from the lies and delusions with which the world
endeavours to seduce us. Father Ho Lung knows this and, as
we shall see, he knows something even greater, something that
shows us not only the secret of life but the secret of love.

Maurice Baring, a great friend of G. K. Chesterton and Hilaire
Belloc, was, like Father Ho Lung, a convert to the Catholic
faith. He wrote the words quoted above about the acceptance
of suffering as he was struggling with the debilitating effects
of Parkinson's disease, the affliction that would eventually kill
him.

Although acceptance of suffering is a choice, suffering itself
is not. We are all doomed to suffer, whether we like it or not
or whether we choose it or not. Suffering is not a choice, it is a
gift. It is given to each of us. Most of us, to be sure, would rather
not have it. Most of us do our best to avoid it. Since, however,
it is unavoidable, the wise learn to accept it. It is, however, only
the holy who openly embrace it and seek it out. It is the holy
who understand the true secret of love as well as the true secret
of life, which is not merely the acceptance of suffering but the
joyful embrace of all suffering, not simply our own but that of
our neighbor, and of our God. This is the ultimate secret that
is revealed by the Suffering Christ and by those of his disciples, such as Father Ho Lung and the Missionaries of the Poor,
who take up their crosses to follow Him. Suffering, properly
understood in its Christ-like simplicity and complexity, is to be
not only endured but enjoyed, not in any sordid masochistic
sense but in the liberating sense of the lessons it teaches and the
riches it bestows.

Scripture is awash with examples of souls being ennobled
and enriched by the experience, acceptance and embrace of
suffering. One of the most powerful is the example of the two

thieves crucified on either side of Christ on Golgotha. These two thieves can be said to represent the whole of humanity. Both are sinners who have harmed their neighbors through acts of selfishness. Both are guilty of the crimes for which they are being punished and deserve the death that is meted out to them in justice. Neither can escape from their suffering. They are like the rest of us. They are, however, very different in the way that they view their own suffering and that of the innocent Man who is suffering with them. The bad thief does not care about justice. He does not feel guilty for the suffering he has caused to others. He wishes only to escape his own suffering. He scorns the innocent Man who is his God as he had scorned his fellow men who were his neighbors. Indeed God is his neighbor, nailed to the cross beside him for the sins the bad thief has committed. Insofar as the bad thief had caused suffering to his neighbor, he had caused suffering to his God. The good thief knows that he is as much a sinner as the bad thief and that he deserves equal punishment in justice for the suffering he has inflicted on his neighbor. The difference is that he accepts his suffering and begs his God, and by extension his neighbor, to forgive him. In accepting his suffering he is accepting the forgiveness. In the acceptance of both he is accepted by God into His Kingdom. Thus the acceptance of suffering is the precursor of the joy that is its consequence.

The acceptance of suffering may indeed be the secret of life, as Maurice Baring's fictional priest tells us, but the joyful service of Christ on the Cross is the secret of love. This is the secret that Father Ho Lung and the Missionaries of the Poor are seeking to share with the suffering of the world.

Chapter One

FROM BUDDHA TO CHRIST

"BORN of a humble and simple origin, yet destined for a great and immeasurable task. Born under the shadow of anonymity, yet sealed to be a light in an era of indomitable darkness. Born concealed from the face of humanity, yet set to shine forth the light of a new civilization, a civilization of love, a civilization of the children of God. This is Fr. Richard Ryan Ho Lung."[1] Such are the words of Brother Arnold, one of more than five hundred brothers of the Missionaries of the Poor (MOP), who have joined Father Ho Lung in a life of poverty.

It seems appropriate to commence our journey in the footsteps of the Founder of the Missionaries of the Poor by seeing him in the light of those who have followed him in the hardship of real life, of those who have embraced a life of poverty, chastity, obedience and free service to the poorest of the poor. Father Ho Lung is truly an extraordinary man; a man who has been blessed with extraordinary gifts. It is, therefore, decorous to commence with an evocation of the enormity of the man's achievement before we proceed to the humble place at which his life began.

Father Ho Lung founded the Brothers of the Poor, as they

---

1. Brother Arnold, unpublished manuscript.

were then called, in 1981, with a handful of disciples, half of whom would leave soon afterwards to pursue a less challenging life. Today, a little over thirty years later, the Missionaries of the Poor have missions in Jamaica, Haiti, Uganda, Kenya, India, the Philippines, Indonesia and the United States. Their success they hope to be recognized officially by the Vatican with the bestowal upon them of the status of Pontifical Institute, the Church's recognition that a religious congregation has become the Catholic equivalent of a global corporation. Continuing this intriguing and perhaps inappropriate and irreverent analogy, Father Ho Lung, a child of poor Chinese immigrants to Jamaica, is the equivalent of a CEO of a multinational missionary corporation! And yet this corporation, or institute, has no employees because nobody earns a salary. Furthermore, Father Ho Lung, its CEO, or Founder-Father, earns the same as everyone else: nothing. This is a global corporation with a difference, one which offers itself in free service to those who are poorest. The MOP does not accept any payment for its work because its "customers" are not able to pay. Amazingly, and some might say miraculously, this "business model" has proved a resounding success, with young men from India, Africa, the Philippines and the Caribbean desiring to join the "company" of Brothers. Father Richard Ho Lung, born of humble and simple origin, under the shadow of anonymity, in the poverty of Jamaica, has come a long way.

*   *   *

Richard Ryan Ho Lung was born on September 17, 1939, in Richmond St. Mary in Jamaica, on the feast of St. Robert Bellarmine, the Jesuit and Doctor of the Church who had been canonized nine years earlier by Pope Pius XI. The date was

perhaps portentous considering Father Ho Lung's later vocation to the Jesuit Order. His parents were Chinese Buddhists
who had migrated to Jamaica several years earlier. His father,
Willie Ho Lung (Seang Ho Lung Quee), had been born in Macao
on February 1, 1898, but came to Jamaica in the footsteps of his
own father who had migrated earlier. A quiet man, steady and
hardworking, he was converted to Catholicism in Hong Kong
in 1969, at the age of seventy-one, and died five years later, on
November 6, 1974. Richard's mother, Janet Ho Lung (Seang
Cheng Shue Cheng), was twenty-three years younger than her
husband, being born in Kowloon on April 28, 1921. Their marriage was an arranged one, as was customary. Janet Ho Lung
was only sixteen when the first of their children, Loretta, was
born on December 14, 1937, and was eighteen when Richard,
their first son, was born. Two other children would follow a
few years later: Theresa on September 30, 1946, and Michael on
November 21, 1947.

Gentle, sweet, thoughtful, artistic, and a lover of nature,
Janet Ho Lung was converted to Catholicism in 1950, at the age
of twenty-nine, when her son was ten-years-old, and died of
cancer at the tender age of forty-six, on February 5, 1968. "My
relationship with my mother was a very deep one," remembers
Father Ho Lung, "and my father was always there, but he was
more remote."[2] His mother could hardly speak English but
managed to communicate very well with her neighbours. "She
possessed great dignity and simplicity, kindness and warmth."
His father, in contrast, was "a quiet strong presence" to his wife
and children, though "somewhat of a dreamer with a far rang-
ing mind on matters of geopolitics." He worked hard all day in

---

2. Unless stated otherwise, all quotes by Father Ho Lung are from interviews given to the author in Kingston, Jamaica, between March 2011 and
January 2012.

their little grocery store but never seemed to have much to show for his labors. Willie Ho Lung's faithfulness and strong sense of justice have remained with Father Ho Lung, particularly his father's advice to never forget the poor people of Jamaica, no matter what. "Concern for the poor was very deep in his heart and mind."

During the first years of Richard's life, the family practiced Buddhism. His mother lit candles, burnt incense, chanted in Chinese, and distributed little ceremonial cakes for the family to eat. She insisted on the children being prayerful and often took them to the riverside where they were made to sit in silence while she asked them questions intended to prompt meditation in their young minds. "We'd listen to the wind and watch it as it stirred in the trees or the water," Father Ho Lung recalled. "We were led to really wonder about the mysteries of nature." On other occasions, their mother got her children to pound on the earth, to feel it, to try to understand that the earth gives life, trees, flowers, and fruits of all different kinds. "The mystery of water and earth was very much a part of our upbringing. She loved nature herself. We were always giving thanks."

Father Ho Lung credited his Buddhist childhood for developing in him a sense of mystery and a great respect for nature. "Buddhism taught us to be one with our environment and those around us. It taught us to desire nothing we do not possess but to appreciate the mysterious presence of an unknown God and the beauty and harmony within nature. We learned to meditate and seek enlightenment. Buddhism makes you someone who seeks and therefore, in many ways, it really leads to Christianity in a most wonderful way."

On one occasion he and his elder sister, Loretta, went next door to the home of their paternal grandparents and watched as their mother chanted and beat the ground with branches to ward off evil spirits that she believed had been the cause of a nightmare she'd had the previous night. Their grandparents' house was much larger than their own somewhat cramped home. It had spacious rooms, a verandah, and a piano. In spite of such apparent opulence, Willie and Janet were poor and the children often went without shoes, though Father Ho Lung didn't recall this as a major inconvenience, considering the Jamaican climate and the carefree existence that he enjoyed in the countryside. He and Loretta played in the surrounding fields and woods, paddled in small pools, and caught minnows, which they called "janga."

"As a little boy in the country we played a lot by the riverside, which was just across the street from where we lived, and played hide and seek, picked mangos from the trees and romped with our neighbors, but it was a very free life and a very happy life in many ways. Yes, it was carefree although we were poor. We were not conscious of being poor nor did we worry about it. People were very kind. Everybody shared. Ladies who sold mangos and sweet substance on the side road would always give us something if we were hungry. I would pick plums from the trees. Then we also found that people would come to our little store when they were in trouble. We used the word 'trust.' We would allow them to trust a little bit for the oil or the sugar or the fish or whatever they needed."

In spite of such poverty, or perhaps because of it, Father Ho Lung remembers his childhood as a time of halcyon and arcadian peace, filled with friendly faces and set against a picturesque landscape, Sarah and Nora, "the Jamaican women who cared for us as their own children"; "the gregariousness of Jamaican blacks, the beautiful and lively revival music, the friendliness and spontaneity of those in our poor neighborhood, the religious nature of our people, and the magnificent presence of the Almighty in the mountains, hills and rivers." All of these memories and experiences of childhood are part of what Father Ho Lung describes as "the soulscape of myself and my family."[3]

Richard attended school in the north Jamaican town of Highgate St. Mary in these early years but, when he was seven, the family moved to Kingston, Jamaica's capital, so that he and his siblings could get a proper education. His father rented a small grocery store at 42 Old Hope Road, which became their new home. Although he and his siblings were unhappy with the move to the big city, they adjusted well and began their education in earnest. After a year at Camperdown high school, Richard moved to Alvernia preparatory school, where he was deeply influenced by the teachings of Sister Mary Elizabeth and the Franciscan sisters, who taught him about Jesus' love for the poor. He and his family were as poor as they had been in the countryside and he recalls, without embarrassment, that he was sixteen before he first wore underwear. He had only one pair of pants, which he wore until they were utterly tattered. He walked barefoot to school, where he regularly went without lunch. At home, one small cup of rice was often passed around for dinner to be shared by the entire family. "No electricity, lack of food and even water, the pit toilet, none of these created shame or anxiety in our family. There was worry, but the love connection between us overrode our fear," Father Ho Lung recalled.

Richard and his siblings befriended two other Chinese families who were considerably wealthier and lived in a much larger house nearby. The children of the two families played happily

---

3. Father Ho Lung's memoir in *Missionaries of the Poor 25th Jubilee: The Official Pictorial Magazine*, Kingston, Jamaica: Missionaries of the Poor, 2006, p. 18.

together and Richard does not recall that the disparity in wealth caused any problems or friction. Even at Christmas, when he and his siblings received only one present each whereas their friends received many more, he did not recall feelings of envy coming between them. "This revealed from an early age his lack of concern for status," wrote his biographer, Fr. Kenneth Payne, "and may well have helped to pave the way for events later in life."[4] Father Ho Lung remembered his mother gathering him and Loretta around the bed to tell them of the family's struggles to make ends meet:

> She said, "I want you to know and want you to understand that we are poor people, but you know we love you," and at that time we understood in a very, very deep way what was really the true meaning of life. My father came in and he said, "You know I want you both to remember one thing, that it doesn't really matter whether you're rich or you're poor. Those things don't matter. And if you're poor and people don't want to be your friend then they shouldn't be your friend. They're not worthy of it." And he said to me, "There are certain values in life that you must not forget, and that is to learn to commit yourself to people for who they are."

These words of parental wisdom had a liberating effect on the two children. "We didn't care who we were or what we were, the fact that we had a latrine toilet and that we bathed from pans of water rather than having a shower. We were just joyful and glad and happy just the way we were."

In a childhood filled mostly with joy, the saddest moment of

---

4. Kenneth Payne, *Joy for All?: The Life and Work of Father Richard Ho Lung*, Peterborough, England: Fast Print Publishing, 2011, p. 12.

Father Ho Lung's childhood was a neighbor girl's descent into immorality:

> "We lived right next to people who were very, very poor, and I remember that there was a girl in the neighborhood. She was about four or five years older than me, but she was always very nice and that's what was distressing. She was about fourteen-years-old and she began to dress in a way that disturbed me and my sister. I was about ten-years-old and didn't understand these things at that time. I came to understand because I was fond of her and so was my sister. She was clearly advertising herself. The men in the area began to laugh at her and called her a whore. I didn't know the word but I got a sense of its meaning from the derisory attitude of the men. So I went up to her and asked her whether she was a whore. She looked at me and started to cry. She told me never to call her that again. I said, 'But are you?' And she said, 'I do bad things.' I said, 'But you don't have to do those bad things.'" As time went on, he began to realize that they were growing apart and that she had chosen another path. "Then she began to become very flagrant in her profession, and I got really mad. I began to really quarrel with her and went to my mother and father. 'This is what is happening,' I said. 'This is what is happening here. Can you do anything about it? Can't you tell her?'" His father told him that nothing could be done: "These things happen to people. You just have to accept it." More than sixty years later, Father Ho Lung still recalled the memory as "a very sad moment in my life."

Meanwhile at Alvernia preparatory school, the young Buddhist boy was being taught by Sister Mary Elizabeth, an Irish-American from New York. "What really drew me to Sister Mary Elizabeth was her tremendous love of music," he remembered. She used to dance and sing. "When Irish Eyes Are Smiling" was a favorite and she told the children that it was the greatest song that had ever been written. "Danny Boy" was another song that she sang often. "She would be at the piano banging away while she danced and all the rest of it. She was a real source of mystery to me, and had such a love for the children. She protected us. She watched over us. She taught us everything that she knew. She wanted to pass the knowledge on to us, and that was very powerful to me." She told stories about the life of Christ, of whom Richard knew very little at the time, "of His tenderness and how He took care of the sick, the blind, the deaf, and how He welcomed little children to Himself and was crucified because of our sins and our weaknesses." Whereas Buddhism was impersonal, with no clear indication of a divinity defined and visible and real, Christ was a real life Person: "I can't say that I felt dissatisfied with my Buddhism but once we were told about Christ by the Franciscan sisters you just felt enthralled and satisfied and just overwhelmed by this Christ. Christ who walked upon the waters. Christ who multiplied loaves. Christ who died upon the Cross. The sisters talked about Christ in a way that we really understood."

I asked Father Ho Lung about the enduring influence of oriental and Franciscan nature mysticism on the spirituality of the Missionaries of the Poor. I greatly admired the way that the Brothers had turned their communities into beautiful places with landscaped gardens, mango and other fruit-bearing trees, aviaries, aquaria, and livestock. I wondered whether there was a correlation between the Buddhist respect and love for nature and the similar Franciscan charism. I was thinking of the nature mysticism of Father Ho Lung's mother and the beauty of Saint Francis' "Canticle to Brother Sun." I also couldn't help seeing a parallel between Saint Francis' stripping himself naked of all his worldly goods and walking into the woods to wed his Lady Poverty and Father Ho Lung's similar stripping himself of all worldly comforts to serve the poorest of the poor. In spite of his Jesuit background, I wondered about this apparent Franciscan dimension to his spirituality. Was there a connection between his childhood Buddhism and the subsequent influence of the Franciscan sisters and has this found expression in the spirituality of the Missionaries of the Poor?

"There is a real connection," Father Ho Lung replied, "but only upon reflection. You can see the way we were brought up was really to love nature and to respect it and to understand how precious every bit of creation is. And Jamaica is a country just filled with so much beauty, so much natural beauty. But also the people. We learned at a very, very tender age to respect people of all ages. I think the Franciscan aspect of nature also came in, because Sister Mary Elizabeth, this wonderful woman, taught us about caring for flowers, little violets and various tropical plants. She used to tell us the names of them, and she would have us work in the garden as part of our classes. So you're right. The Buddhism led us in that direction, and Jamaica being so naturally beautiful, and then the dearest of teachers being so respectful of nature as Christians; all of this set the background for what is now MOP spirituality."

Looking back, Father Ho Lung laughs as he recalls the moment that Sister Mary Elizabeth told him and Loretta that they needed to become Catholics. She did so with evangelical zeal and pre-Vatican II bluntness, dropping a hint that was as subtle as a bombshell. "Look," she said, "you've been coming to the school and you haven't become Catholic. Do you know what happens to people who don't become Catholic? After they die, they go to hell. Do you want to go to hell?"

As Father Ho Lung laughed at the recollection of the memory, I commented that this was certainly a good old-fashioned way of winning converts.

"It was perfect though," he responded. "It was very effective. We were a bit scared, and we agreed to become Catholics . . . but really happily. It's just that we didn't know how to approach it ourselves."

Richard and Loretta were duly baptized into the Catholic Church on May 6, 1948, with the blessing of their parents. As already noted, their mother would be received into the Church two years later, whereas their father would not finally be baptized until 1969, just five years before his death.

Shortly after his reception, Richard remembered walking past the school chapel. He had been taught to bow as he passed by the entrance but this time, seeing the light near the tabernacle, he went in. "There was something so sacred about the whole chapel and the sense of the presence of God. I knelt down, and I prayed. I felt very deeply the presence of the Lord, and knew that this was what I wanted."

Little could the young convert have known it at the time but he was embarking upon a lifelong love affair.

Chapter Two
....

THE CALL AND FALL
OF THE JESUITS

I love my fellow Jesuits to this day as part of myself,
and I pray for the Society of Jesus that it be restored
to St. Ignatius' intention that we be the standard of
Christ against the prince of this world.

—Father Ho Lung,
in *Missionaries of the*
Poor 25th Jubilee

EARLY in 1950, Richard applied to enter St. George's College, a Jesuit-run high school in Kingston. At the time, it was the only Catholic high school for boys in the city. Many of his friends encouraged him to apply, telling him that it was a great school and that it welcomed Chinese students and the poor. He also heard nothing but praise of the Jesuit teachers, who were described to him as being great men. Spurred on by this positive peer pressure, he desired greatly to be admitted but failed the entrance examination. "I failed because I didn't know what entrance exams were. We were really not prepared. We were just playful kids. We never studied even while we were with Sister. We just enjoyed everything that she had to offer but we really didn't study."

At this point, any ordinary child would have accepted his fate. Richard Ho Lung, however, was no ordinary child. He was not about to take no for an answer. "Even as a little boy I was a little daring," he recalled. He approached the headmaster, Father Charles MacMullen, whom he remembered as "a beautiful priest," and told him that he wanted to come to St. George's College. "But you failed the exam," the priest replied. The ten-year-old responded that he would still like to be admitted. "But you haven't passed," the priest repeated, though the child noticed that the priest was smiling, perhaps charmed by the sheer chutzpah and persistence of the boy. "I want to come to this school, because this is the right school for me," the irrepressible child explained. "Oh, really?" said the priest. "Okay, you can come."

Thus, against the odds and in spite of such an unpromising start, the boy who failed the entrance exam was admitted to St. George's College. "They put me in with the brightest students. I was at the bottom of the class all the time. But I will never forget the warmth of Father Charles MacMullen. He was very strict, very firm, but he always had a smile on his face." It seems indeed that the headmaster retained a soft spot for the precocious failure who had charmed his way into his school. He befriended the boy, taking him to one side on a regular basis to find out how he was doing. "Dickie, Dickie," he would say, "come here. Let's have a little chat." More than sixty years later, Father Ho Lung still seemed astonished that this busy priest, the headmaster of a school of several hundred students, could find time for "little chats" with such an unpromising student. "I could not understand why, because I was really the biggest dunce of all. Yet he always had special attention to offer me. His warmth and friendship were truly inspirational."

Father Gerald Hennessey, who taught Richard biology,

was another inspirational presence at St. George's. Father Hennessey's passion for botany and zoology was so powerful and infectious that Father Ho Lung considers him an important influence, alongside the Buddhist and Franciscan presence in his childhood, on the formation of the nature mysticism at the heart of MOP spirituality. "We began to study the intricacies of the body and the intricacies of nature; the veins and all the different stems of plants and the colors and the differences between them. We learned to really enjoy the differences that there are between things and the beauty that there is in the differences." He also remembered watching Sophocles' play, *Oedipus Rex*, under the direction of another Jesuit teacher, Father Frank Shea. This experience nurtured the love of literature, which would come to academic fruition in the receipt of a doctorate many years later and subsequently in his returning to St. George's College as a teacher of literature in the 1970s.

The conviviality and *joie de vivre*, which shine so brightly in the elderly Father Ho Lung, were also present in the teenage boy growing in his faith. He and Loretta made friends easily and went frequently to the beach and to the cinema. On his return from the movie theater, he often headed straight to his mother's room where, as often as not, she would be found reading a book, and proceeded to tell her all about the film he had just seen, making her laugh by mimicking the characters. He and Loretta would go to dances, which Richard enjoyed very much, though his relationship with the girls with whom he danced was always platonic. After school on Fridays and all day on Saturdays, he and his older sister helped their father in the grocery store, sometimes working until as late as seven in the evening. He also spent time playing with his two younger siblings, telling them stories and teaching them to do handstands and somersaults on their parents' bed. In quieter moments,

Richard's love of nature found expression in the keeping of tropical fish in a homemade tank at the back of the store.

*   *   *

On August 17, 1951, Hurricane Charlie hit Jamaica, causing extensive damage in Kingston, Port Royal and Morant Bay. A category three storm, it would become the worst natural disaster of the century in Jamaica, claiming the lives of more than 150 people and causing $50 million in damage to property. The entire Ho Lung family huddled together in one room to weather the storm. The wind and rain "sounded like millions of nails dropping from the sky" onto the zinc roof of their house, the windows rattled noisily and threateningly, and there were buckets and containers everywhere to catch the water coming through the ceiling. There was a real fear that the roof and ceiling would collapse upon the family, burying them alive, and they joined in prayer, aloud to Christ, that they might be spared.[1]

The Ho Lung family survived the storm, but many of Jamaica's poor saw their poverty increase, or worse. While studying at St. George's, Richard often visited the yards near the school and witnessed the incredible destitution and poverty. He was robbed one night coming from a ghetto theatre. "I was in tears, not at the thought that I had lost anything valuable, but at the plight to which poverty had driven those young boys in their teens to loot and steal."

Such episodes reminded Richard of the grinding poverty and penury that many of his fellow Jamaicans endured daily. There was a stark contrast between the life on the streets and

---

1. Payne, op. cit., pp. 12–13.

the relatively affluent culture of the college and its students. Although he was never tempted temperamentally to follow the path of least resistance, allowing himself to be seduced by worldliness, or the lure and allure of materialism, he continued to be helped on his path to sanctity by the positive example of the Jesuits who taught him. His gratitude, undiminished across the decades, is evident in the enthusiasm with which he recounts his experience of a Jesuit education in the pre-Vatican II calm that preceded the following decade's storm:

> I loved my high school days. The Jesuits were an astonishing group of men. They were totally dedicated to the schoolboys. They were friendly and warm, strict and demanding. They possessed a vision of service that captured my heart and mind. Fathers Bill Raftery, Gerry Hennessey, Leo Quinlan and Paul Hayes were four of such men. They were servants of the Lord and servants of Jamaica.
>
> The Jesuits were a family. I saw it in the uniformity of their white habits, their oneness as a community in prayer and work, their dedication to Christ and the Church, and their love of the schoolboys. They could have been living lives of wealth, ease and success; so intelligent and convivial were they. Instead, they were on a mission to educate and pass on the Catholic faith to us Jamaican boys.[2]

Encouraged by the "wonderful example" set for him by his Jesuit teachers and singling out Father MacMullen and Father Raftery, in particular, for fostering his vocation, Richard felt, at the age of fourteen, the call to a priestly vocation with the Society of Jesus.

---

2. Father Ho Lung's memoir, op. cit., p. 19.

Ironically, Richard ended his time at St. George's College as he had begun it, by failing an exam. As he had failed the entrance exam eight years earlier, he also failed the English exam that every student needed to pass in order to graduate. Perhaps his mother's practical illiteracy in English contributed to his failure. Although she was an avid reader, she read in her native Cantonese and was unable to read English. He re-took the exam and was eventually able to graduate. Just as the boy who failed the entrance exam to a Jesuit school would go on to become a Jesuit, so the boy who failed the English exam in order to graduate from high school would go on to receive a Master's degree in English literature and would teach English at university level.

After graduating from St. George's College, Richard spent a short time working for British West Indian Airways before joining the New England Province of the Society of Jesus in Shadowbrook, Massachusetts, on the Feast of the Assumption (August 15), 1959. He was a few weeks shy of his twentieth birthday. His father, who would not become a Catholic until ten years later, accepted his son's vocation, whereas his mother, who had converted almost ten years earlier, was angered by his decision and refused to speak to him for many months afterwards. The inherent irony was due to the detached and somewhat distant relationship that Richard had with his father, as compared to the closeness of his relationship with his mother. One can empathize with the mother's disappointment at her son's leaving for the Jesuit seminary in the United States and her fear that she might see very little of him in the future.

In stark contrast to the exemplary Jesuits at St. George's College, Richard soon discovered that everything was not as it should be, or as he imagined it would be, among the Jesuits in Boston. He was destined as the sixties "progressed" to see the dark underbelly of the Society of Jesus as it sank into the murk of modernism. The worst experience of the early days of his novitiate, however, had nothing to do with modernism and everything to do with the supercilious attitude of his Speech Master. This arrogant priest reprimanded Ho Lung for his Jamaican accent, telling him that he would never succeed in either public speaking or the priesthood unless he could shake off his Caribbean roots. Mortified by the insult, the young seminarian responded by working ever harder at his studies, earning Master's degrees in English Literature and Philosophy, a Doctorate in Humanities, and completing graduate studies in Theology. He went on to teach at Boston College, the University of the West Indies, and also at St. George's College.

Looking back on his early days as a Jesuit seminarian, Father Ho Lung remembered happy and exciting days with no hint of the troubles to come. "Everything was given to me as I threw myself into the Jesuit life: brilliant professors, warm and loving fellowship in community with young Jesuits, teachers and spiritual directors."[3] He stressed, in particular, his indebtedness to the Master of Novices, Father John Post, who directed him in the Ignatian Spiritual Exercises during the first year of his seminary training. Above all, he was influenced by Father William Burke, whom he described as "a father and friend to me" throughout the years of his Juniorate, Philosophate, and Theologate. "Not only did my spiritual father spiritually direct me but also taught me to discern life in the Church. He also interested me in psychology and the spiritual nature of man. I drank of every word he said to me, and up to this day I am guided by his wisdom. We shared deeply in days of distress and days of glory."[4]

---

3. Ibid., p. 19.
4. Ibid.

Father Ho Lung dates the "days of distress" to 1964, when he realized that "a terrible storm of change was upon us":

> It was relentless and without discrimination. Religious life would be humanized to the point of losing its spirituality. All of us Jesuits were being attacked by the evil one who hates those who work for the standard of Christ. Whereas the clericalism within religious life required change because of its separation from the reality of people's suffering and daily struggles, as Jesuits we also seemed to have lost our deep Christocentric commitment.[5]

The warning signs had been there during the previous year when the celebrated English Jesuit, Father Martin D'Arcy, visited the juniorate in Boston at which Richard was studying. At the time, Father D'Arcy was probably the most famous and most celebrated Jesuit in the English-speaking world. He has since been described as "perhaps England's foremost Catholic public intellectual from the 1930s until his death [in 1978]."[6] He had a reputation for ushering high profile converts into the Church. He received Evelyn Waugh into the Church in 1930, was a valued spiritual adviser to Dorothy L. Sayers and W. H. Auden, a friend of J.R.R. Tolkien, and was immortalized in fiction by Muriel Spark, herself a Catholic convert, when she said of one of her characters in *The Girls of Slender Means* that "he could never make up his mind between suicide and an equally drastic course of action known as Father D'Arcy." In the novella, written in 1963, the year that D'Arcy visited the Boston seminary, Spark described D'Arcy as "a Jesuit philosopher who had

---

5. Ibid.
6. Richard Harp, "A Conjurer at the Christmas Party," Times Literary Supplement, December 11, 2009.

the monopoly for converting the English intellectuals."[7] He is also believed to have been the model for the character of Father Mowbray in Waugh's novel, *Brideshead Revisited.* D'Arcy wrote several influential books, including *The Mind and Heart of Love*, published by T. S. Eliot at Faber & Faber in 1945. Apart from his celebrity status, D'Arcy had also been the Provincial of the English Province of the Jesuits from 1945 until 1950.

At the time of his visit to the seminary, at which Richard Ho Lung was present, Father D'Arcy, then seventy-five-years-old, was a venerable elder of the Jesuit Order. One can imagine the shock, then, when he warned his audience that the Society of Jesus was in jeopardy because of its own wealth and worldli-ness. Father Ho Lung recalls vividly how D'Arcy stood up and told them that he was going to give them the uncomfortable truth, that "the whole thing is going to fall apart" because of the bad habits into which the Jesuits were falling. "The whole thing is going to fall apart because we are too rich," he said. "It can't survive. . . . We're going the wrong way. I see this and I say this in the knowledge that you will be disturbed by what I am saying." He concluded by telling them that "you had better find your way to God." His audience was dumbstruck. "We were all shocked. I was shocked. Our Jesuit superiors were shocked. It was amazing that he had spoken in that manner."

It was indeed shocking. It was also the truth, which would become all too apparent in the months and years ahead.

As the situation worsened, the descent of the Jesuits into worldliness distressed the young seminarian. Ho Lung became alienated from his confreres, most of whom were delighted at the erosion of discipline and doctrine. The lowering and

---

7. Muriel Spark, *The Girls of Slender Means*, New York: New Directions Publishing, 1998 edn., p. 53.

liberalizing of standards "gave a certain façade of freedom," Father Ho Lung remembered, enabling those in the religious life a "freedom" to choose whatever they wanted. This sense of "liberation" became the dominant force among his peers and contemporaries. "We could do whatever we wanted. But I did not think so and I stood out like a sore thumb."

He was outspoken and on one particular occasion issued a plaintive condemnation of the way the Jesuits were reneging on tradition and the Faith: "We have thrown off our habits. We no longer pray daily; we no longer have a life of discipline. There's no sign of austerity and there's no sign of Christ-centeredness." Everything had become arbitrary, "whether we went to classes or not, whether we went to Mass or not, whether we did any work at all to justify the fact that everything was being given to us free of cost." This laissez-faire attitude was popular "because it was appealing to the flesh," and Father Ho Lung remembered his spiritual director advising him that he should go out with women before becoming ordained, "so that you might know what you'll be missing." Ho Lung told him that he had not entered the Jesuits in order to go out with women but because he wanted to give himself fully to a life of service to God. He had embraced celibacy as he had embraced the Cross. He found it disturbing that a Jesuit priest should advise him to experiment with lifestyles inimical to his vocation. "It became a point that fixed in my mind, that my own spiritual director was directing me towards the world."

It was, of course, the so-called "swinging sixties" when it was said that "anything goes." It was disconcerting for Ho Lung to discover that it was also becoming the way of many within the Church. Father Ho Lung remembered that many were following this false sense of freedom. "And it was by the grace of God that I was held back. Something intuitively said, 'no, you can't go that way.' It was false; and even if everybody else said it was right, it was still false. It was wrong. I listened to that intuitive voice and I felt I was meeting God and that God was consenting to my refusal to follow the spirit of the times."

His resolute refusal to join his fellow seminarians in their "liberated" and laissez-faire approach to religious life made him very unpopular. His protests at the contempt with which many treated their studies with disregard for rules and a lack of disciplined prayer caused an uproar. As he sat at the table for meals, his peers would tell him to "get out of here if you don't like this way of life"—"or some would mock and curse me."

As he struggled with these distressing developments, he found invaluable support from his friend and mentor, Father William Burke. Yet even the counsel received from this quarter was disturbing. Echoing the words of Father D'Arcy that "it's all going to fall apart," Father Burke advised Richard that he should consider leaving the Society of Jesus as possibly the only way of surviving spiritually: "to preserve yourself and also to contribute to the Church." He told him not to be afraid of the prospect but to have the courage to do what is necessary, even suggesting that Richard consider starting his own religious order. Above all, he must not give up his vocation. "Whatever you do, do not leave the religious life. Don't ever do that. And if you one day become a priest never stop saying Mass. Say Mass every day. Make a sacrifice of yourself. Stay faithful to the Church and to Christ," he urged. "Don't be afraid. Don't be afraid of suffering. Don't be afraid of suffering no matter what. You're going to be very, very lonely, but persevere."

As Father Ho Lung recalled the words of his late mentor, it was clear that they resonated with undiminished power across the intervening decades. "He has held me together all these years. He preserved my vocation. I listen. I hear him. Every time there are difficulties I turn back to what Bill Burke had said to me. He was a wonderful teacher in spirituality. He opened my heart and mind to many, many things. He kept centering on Christ. He kept centering on Christ."

Father Ho Lung recalled the torments that Father Burke was also going through at the time: "He was so angry at times when he saw what had happened inside the Jesuits. He was very disturbed by what had happened at Boston College." In an effort to stop the rot, he stood for president of the College. "I didn't do it out of pride" he told Father Ho Lung, "but because we have gone the wrong way. We're no longer ministering for the sake of the Father, but are just in it to prove that we're better than everybody else, or equal to other Ivy League schools." Father Burke, like his young protégé, was swimming against the liberal tide. The president's job went to the sort of Jesuit who would continue to oversee Boston College's wholesale abandonment of its Catholic identity and credentials. "He didn't get the job," Father Ho Lung lamented. "He was sort of bypassed and forgotten and rejected by the other Jesuits of the time. He was a brilliant man. He had a doctorate from the Gregorian,[8] and spoke some seven languages. He was really, really a wonderful and a warm human person. Incredibly intense eyes; and you could see the suffering on his face because he loved the Church so much that he felt as though he was losing the very reason for his living. He went through that period of great disturbance and shared it with me. He was sometimes just so angry."

In hindsight, Father Burke's urging of his protégé to leave the Jesuits and embrace a life of suffering seems prophetic.

---

8. Pontifical Gregorian University in Rome; a Jesuit university descended from the Roman College founded by St. Ignatius Loyola in 1551.

At the time, however, Richard could not imagine being anything other than a priest of the Society of Jesus. After years of studies and formation, Richard Ho Lung was ordained to the priesthood on July 4, 1971, at the Holy Trinity Cathedral in Kingston, Jamaica. His training had been tough, not so much due to the rigorous nature of his studies as to the impact of the moral crisis in the Jesuits on his own peace of mind.

> My regency at St. George's College and my theological studies were days living and not-living. I loved the Society of Jesus so much that I could not pull myself out of a period of desolation because it seemed to be falling apart. The desolation lasted for some fifteen years. Always, however, despite sinfulness and doubts, I had a conviction of God's love and my call to be a priest. Christ warmed me in the darkest days with His word and His presence, and His life in the Scriptures never ceased to inspire me. I was jolted out of my lethargy when I became intensely aware of the poverty, social and political problems which were destroying the very soul of Jamaican life.[9]

Whereas many of his contemporaries in the Society of Jesus had abandoned Jesus in order to embrace "society" and its worldly comforts, the newly-ordained priest set forth to embrace the abandoned Jesus among the poorest of the poor.

---

9. Ibid.

Chapter Three

....

IF MUSIC BE THE FOOD OF LOVE . . .

The man that hath no music in himself,
Nor is not moved with concord of sweet sounds,
Is fit for treasons, stratagems, and spoils;
The motions of his spirit are dull as night,
And his affections dark as Erebus.
Let no such man be trusted. Mark the music.
            —Shakespeare, *The Merchant of Venice*

If music be the food of love, play on . . .
            —Shakespeare, *Twelfth Night*

CONSIDERING his uncompromisingly orthodox stance during the years of priestly formation in the United States, the decidedly modern feel of Richard Ho Lung's ordination Mass might seem surprising. The report in the local Catholic newspaper referred to "exotic elements" in the liturgy, most notably the inclusion of liturgical dance at the commencement of proceedings: "Eurhythmic dancing by four young ladies . . . in gold dresses overlaying dark bodices and gay headbands, symbolizing Humanity, Love, Godliness and Strength, opened the ceremony." The report also mentioned that several

27

of Richard's own poems, set to music, formed part of the Mass: "The sound of a bass guitar . . . and clashing cymbals . . . accompanying the poems of the ordinand with musical arrangements by Mapletoft Poulle, and rendered by the Combined Cathedral Choir . . . alternated with the hymns of the regular Mass."[1]

It is tempting to see the "clashing cymbals" as indicative of the clashing symbols in the liturgical form of the ordination Mass, which was described as "a unique occasion in the history of Holy Trinity Cathedral." On the one hand, there was the traditional procession of thirty altar boys and a similar number of clergy and seminarians; on the other, at the front of the procession, immediately behind the cross-bearer, were the four exuberantly clad dancers. As the procession made its way to the altar, the congregation sang the traditional hymn, "Praise My Soul the King of Heaven"; yet after the priests and altar servers had taken their places in the sanctuary, the liturgical dance began, during which "the congregation watched in admiration the graceful evolutions of the dancers." After Richard was vested with stole and chasuble, the choir sang the traditional Latin hymn, "Veni, Creator Spiritus," yet earlier, during the laying on of hands, the choir had sung two of Richard's own poetic compositions, one of which, "Canticle of Canticles," reminiscent of Francis Thompson's "Hound of Heaven," showed the influence of the western literature that Richard was teaching at the University of the West Indies and at St. George's College. The other poem, "I Know," was written in the Jamaican dialect.

Following the ordination ceremony, the offertory hymn, "A Child Finds," and the communion hymns, "Give Praise to the Lord" and "Jesus Gave 'ternal Life," were also composed by

---

1. Details of Father Ho Lung's ordination ceremony are taken from the report in *Catholic Opinion*, (Kingston), July 9, 1971.

Father Ho Lung. Clearly the newly-ordained priest had a musical gift to bring to his ministry.

There is, in fact, a paradox, or perhaps a tension, and even an irony, in the connection between the orthodoxy of Father Ho Lung's beliefs and the vernacular style of his music. Does the universal aspect of his orthodoxy clash with the consciously local dimension of his music? Does Father Ho Lung's embrace of the pop culture of his native Jamaica contradict the high calling of Catholic civilization? Conversely, could it be argued that the composing of music that resonates with indigenous popular culture is a legitimate expression of inculturation and subsidiarity? It is well to address these issues now to avoid confusion later.

It is also well, in the interests of full disclosure, for the author to confess his own principles and predilections with regard to music, particularly with regard to the use of music in the liturgy.

I readily confess that my initial contact with Father Ho Lung and the Missionaries of the Poor was a real challenge to my preconceptions. I was affronted by the apparent disconnection between the orthodoxy and sanctity, on the one hand, and the exuberance of the Caribbean music and rhythms on the other hand. My own experience of the sort of Jesuit heroes who had resisted the modernist revolution in the Society of Jesus, such as Fathers Fessio, Schall, Hardon, and Pacwa, suggested that Father Ho Lung would be as traditional as they in his approach to the liturgy and liturgical music. In Europe and the United States, liturgical dance, electric guitars, folk "hymns," and hand-clapping are a sure sign that the modernist rot had set in. Thus, it is difficult for a European or American to read a description of Father Ho Lung's ordination Mass and equate it with the resolute heroism with which he confronted the modernist ascendancy of the Jesuits. Was Father Ho Lung endeavoring to meld together two incompatible and ultimately inimical approaches to spirituality and the liturgy, or was there an overarching harmony between his music and his mission that I was missing?

While I'm in confessional mode, I should perhaps confess that my own view of the liturgy is modeled on that of Cardinal Ratzinger (Pope Benedict XVI), as expressed with sublime eloquence in *The Spirit of the Liturgy*. I believe that the priest should be facing the same way as the congregation, *ad orientem*, so that we are all one in prayer, turning toward the Lord, as opposed to the priest facing the opposite direction, *versus populum* (the priest versus the people!) with a "table" between himself and the congregation, much like a public speaker addressing an audience, and with the "throne" on which he sits placed in the center of the sanctuary in the place where the tabernacle used to be (the removal of Jesus to make way for the priest!). Furthermore, I like to kneel for communion. I like altar rails. I like to receive Our Lord's *corpus* on my tongue. I am very comfortable with the Old Rite, or as it is now called, the Extraordinary Form of the Mass. And as for liturgical music, my preference is for Gregorian chant and the Polyphony of Palestrina, Tallis, and Byrd.

I will make a further confession: I have come to really enjoy and appreciate the music of Father Ho Lung. I like the early recordings, particularly "Sinner" and "Babylon a Catch Me"; I like some of the musical numbers, such as "Take My Life," "I Will Serve You" and "You are My Destiny"; I find the irrepressible joy and jollity of "Blessed Be the People" and "Enter into Jerusalem" irresistible, and Father Ho Lung's musical adaptation of the Canticle of Daniel leaves me speechless with delight! And I will make another confession. I even enjoy Father Ho Lung's "Caribbean Mass," especially the infectiously memorable "Alleluia" and the rambunctious vivaciousness of the "Our Father."

Perhaps the question I posited earlier ought to be redirected towards myself. Am I as guilty as Father Ho Lung of endeavoring to meld together two incompatible and ultimately inimical approaches to spirituality and the liturgy? Should I address the plank in my own eye before I suggest that Father Ho Lung has a splinter in his? Or, perhaps, is there an overarching harmony between Father Ho Lung's music and mission that I have finally managed to see? To continue with the biblical metaphor, had I gone searching for the splinter in Father Ho Lung's eye only to discover that he had removed the plank from mine?

The answers to these questions emerged with time and prayer as I came to know Father Ho Lung better, and most especially from my own discussions with him as I grappled to understand this musical paradox at the heart of his mission.

Interviewing Father Ho Lung, along with Father Brian, one of the original founding Brothers of the MOP, I confronted the apparent contradiction between the Jesuit seminarian who had rejected the spirit of the age with which his fellow Jesuits were besotted, and yet, at the same time, seemed to engage the popular culture in the songs that he was writing.

"What made it actually consistent with the priest rejecting the culture of the times," said Father Brian, "is that the music that Father was writing was an association with the poor and an identification with them. It was an effort to bring the Church into closer communion with the suffering of the poor. Father saw what was happening with the poor and the music was a way of connecting with them in their suffering."[2] Father Brian

---

2. All quotes from Father Brian Kerr are from my interviews with him in Kingston, Jamaica, between March 2011 and January 2012.

then quoted some lines from one of Father Ho Lung's songs to illustrate his point: *when buried under the mango tree, the board drifts out in the storm like sea, oh Lord have mercy.* "That song just came out of Father while he was walking among poor people. A woman had lost her husband; he was a fisherman and the boat drifted out to sea and he was buried under the mango tree." Father Brian also explained the use of the vernacular and patois in the songs as a means of "trying to bring the Church in Jamaica to a place where the Church was not at the time willing to be." And then Father Brian said something that really struck home. "It was like Mother Theresa and her sisters going out to the ghettos of Calcutta and wearing saris."

It was as though a light had switched on in my mind. Of course! Mother Teresa and the Missionaries of Charity wore saris so that they could get closer to the poor whom they served. In order to serve the poor more fully you have to meet them where they are. As far as possible, you have to live the life of the poor. You have to become poor yourself. If the poor in the ghettos of Calcutta wore saris, the Missionaries of Charity would wear saris. If the poor in the ghettos of Kingston relate to the reality around them through music, the Missionaries of the Poor would reach out to them through the power of music. And then, as if another light had switched on in my mind, I realized that I was also a child of the ghetto, in the sense that I was brought up in a poor area of the East End of London. The culture in which I was raised was effectively agnostic. My parents didn't practice any faith. If asked, they would have called themselves Christian but their Christianity did not involve any practical commitment to prayer or to Christ. We never went to church. We never prayed.

I had no connection to organized religion, and I, too, was reached through the power of music. An East End boy did not

listen to classical music but I liked various genres of popular
music. The only Christianity to which I was exposed as a boy
was the Gospel music of Elvis and Jim Reeves. This whetted
my appetite. It fed my desire for more. As a teenager, I could
not and would not have listened to the polyphonous splendor
of Thomas Tallis or William Byrd, but listening to Elvis led me
in the direction in which, eventually, I would desire other types
of religious music. The music met me where I was and led me
in the direction in which I needed to go, albeit by small, falter-
ing steps. I realized that what Father Ho Lung was doing with
the Caribbean music was exactly the same. He was meeting the
poor where they were because you can't meet them anywhere
else. I also realized that my initial reaction against such music
was a lack of respect for the poor and a supercilious arrogance
akin to the Jesuit Speech Master who had told Father Ho Lung
that he would never succeed as long as he had a Jamaican
accent. I was mortified and at the same time enlightened. I
finally understood.

"It was part of the whole movement to stir in people's hearts
the gospel message to reach out to the poor," Father Brian continued. "So the apparent paradox is rooted in the fact that the
music was actually a means of reaching the poor people. Using
their language. The issues of justice being expressed, of the tenderness of the poor, their suffering, the joy of the Caribbean life.
The music conveyed a lot of that Caribbean joy, the rhythms of
the people, and connected it to the Church."

Father Brian mentioned that some of the Catholic priests and
bishops mocked Father Ho Lung's music because it was vulgar.
They said it had "too much of the local tone of the people, of
the simple consciousness of the ordinary person who was not
really connecting with the Catholic Church or with the high
alignment of the Jesuits of the time." These priests and bishops

who mocked Father Ho Lung, continued Father Brian, "did not understand that it was a desire to bring the gospel to the people and present the gospel in such a way that people are drawn to it, to the music, to the message, to the images that were used in the songs."

Father Ho Lung joined the conversation and explained his feelings of isolation in the Jesuits at the time and how music was an oasis in the spiritual desert: "I would also add that because you were thrown on your own you had to dig in very deeply inside yourself, and to my shock and surprise there was so much there. I mean there was the Lord deep in—I felt the presence of the Lord and I felt Him steering me away from confusion. And, as I said, I was so alone but I began to realize that there's something very, very precious inside of me, which is the interior light. When you think of the interior light you think of it, of course, like Teresa of Avila and all these great, great writers. The interior light."

Apart from doctors of the Church, such as St. Teresa, Father Ho Lung had also studied psychology under the benign influence of his mentor, Father William Burke, and he found that this also helped greatly. "I had done so much reading about Jung who said that at the very depths of man there is a center point where Christ is, the idea of the mandala and so forth. And I began to really see that this is so. Christ is truly within us. We are temples of the Holy Spirit. So the music, being a natural part of myself, I take as being sacred, as all things within me are sacred, although of course there is sin too."

Father Ho Lung also invokes the teaching of the Church on inculturation as a justification for his efforts to evangelize through the music of the poor: "The Second Vatican Council and John Paul II taught that music and language are such a precious part of people's lives, a part of their very selves, that the

Church must inculturate. The Church shouldn't try to force upon the people something that is foreign, that is not of the people themselves." It is, however, important to distinguish between genuine inculturation, as taught by successive popes and as practiced by the Church across the centuries, and the sort of modernist "inculturation" that seeks to undermine orthodox doctrine and authentic tradition. Genuine inculturation has been practiced by the Church throughout her history, as demonstrated by the adoption of extra-scriptural rituals, rooted in local cultures, in the Christian celebration of Christmas, such as the Christmas tree, the Christmas wreath, and the Yule log. The key component of such inculturation is that it affects only the *accidental* aspects of Christmas and not its *essential* meaning.

This understanding of authentic and legitimate inculturation was best encapsulated by St. Gregory the Great at the beginning of the seventh century when he taught of the Church's engagement with different cultures that anything that was not contrary to the Gospel could be preserved. In this spirit, Father Ho Lung's use of Caribbean music is bona fide as long as the meaning of the music is in harmony with the teaching of the Church. Some might see the situation as being more difficult with regard to the use of the rhythms of the Caribbean in the music for the liturgy, especially as recent Church documents have stated explicitly that Gregorian chant has a privileged and preferential position in the hierarchy of musical forms deemed appropriate for liturgical use. It is true also that some forms of music, such as hip-hop, rap, heavy rock, rhythm and blues, and tango, to name but a few, are not suited for the liturgy. No doubt, arguments will continue to rage with regard to whether the music composed by Father Ho Lung for the "Caribbean Mass" is suitable for the supreme sacrifice at the sacred heart of the Church's worship.

Father Ho Lung insists that he takes the teaching on inculturation seriously and that his liturgical music in the Jamaican dialect and with Caribbean rhythms is nothing more—or less—than an open-hearted effort to evangelize the poor. "I really wasn't trying to be rebellious or anything. I was just trying to do what I thought was emerging from myself naturally. And what emerged was this music. I love the language; I love the rhythms. I said okay, let it be." Ho Lung refers to his early liturgical compositions as an effort to speak to the poor in a language that they would understand. "I wrote those early songs because I saw the kids were so bored at Mass. And then to my amazement the kids were really enjoying Mass. They were praying, they were coming on retreats and were working with the poor. So that affirmed it for me. If the tree was beginning to bear fruit, let's go with it."

Anybody who has attended a Mass at which the brothers of the Missionaries of the Poor are singing and swaying, and in some cases dancing, to their Founder Father's liturgical music will agree that "boredom" is the one word that could never be applied to the animating power at work in the spirit of this Caribbean liturgy. On one occasion in 2011, during the inaugural Mass of the new Holy Innocents center, which had been established to tackle the evils of abortion and to help poor pregnant mothers, around thirty brothers, resplendent in white habits, danced and sang in choreographed synchronicity around the altar. It was astonishing to see, at least from the perspective of tradition-oriented Catholics raised on the solemnity and decorum of chant.

After the Mass, I was approached by a young seminarian from the United States, one of about eight seminarians from the Saint Paul Seminary in Minnesota who had come to Jamaica to work with the MOP. He asked me what I had

thought of the exuberant liturgy that we had just experienced.
Well, I said with a smile, it was magnificent but I wouldn't want
to see anything similar in my own parish. Judging by the way
in which the puzzled and perplexed look on the young man's
face evaporated, it seemed that he had been reassured by my
answer. The point is that the Caribbean Mass works when it is
sung by those with the fire and fervor of the Missionaries of the
Poor. The power, the passion, and the Presence of the Spirit of
God are unmistakable. I suspect, however, that its impact and
its suitability for the liturgy will diminish the further that it gets
from the inspired charism of Father Ho Lung and the inspiring zeal of the MOP. Indeed, I can only imagine how tawdry it
would sound if efforts were made to transplant it to an average
Catholic parish in Europe or the United States.

The ultimate purpose of inculturation, as taught by great
popes, such as Leo XIII, Pius XI, Pius XII, and John Paul II is
the spreading of the good news through the adaptation of the
Church to local circumstances. It is the ability of the Church
to speak in tongues. Yet the Church has always taught that
the many tongues are at the service of the One Voice. In this
sense, the Word of the Church is never foreign, wherever it is
preached. We must never forget that the evangelist is never
an imperialist. Only those who do not know the good news
that the evangelist brings can believe that his message is "foreign." Christ and the Gospel are at home everywhere because
Christ is Himself the Home that every man seeks, whether
he knows it or not. In this sense, the native American child
who was taught to sing Palestrina by the Jesuits in the jun-
gles of eighteenth century south America is not the victim of
foreign imperialism but the recipient of a holy gift. The argument for bringing Father Ho Lung's Caribbean Mass to the
ghettos of Jamaica is not, therefore, rooted in a desire to keep

out "foreign" polyphony or "old fashioned" Gregorian chant but, on the contrary, is an effort to reach people who cannot be reached by polyphony or chant. It is meeting the people where they are, not an acceptance that this is the only place that they can be. If Father Ho Lung's music attracts people to the Church it will move them to places where Palestrina will be more accessible.

I hope that the foregoing is not an argument *with* Father Ho Lung but an argument *for* him. I believe, in fact, that he would be in essential agreement with what I have said. Evidence for this can be seen in the development of Father Ho Lung's own music, especially his non-liturgical music, which in recent years has become more complex, incorporating elements of the Broadway musical and even, more recently, elements of classic European opera. Needless to say, he doesn't see the incorporation of these ingredients into his music as "foreign" in the derogatory sense of that word but as a means of raising his own people up, enabling them to ascend to heights that transcend the limitations of the ghetto. What is true of the eighteenth century Amazonian Indian learning Palestrina is true of the twenty-first century Jamaican learning elements of opera.

Ultimately Father Ho Lung's orthodoxy in terms of his preaching and practice of inculturation is not in doubt. Indeed it is confirmed by his affinity for the early Jesuit, St. Francis Xavier, whom he names as his favorite saint. Since St. Francis Xavier is the patron saint of missionaries, and since he led a life of zeal in converting the people of India and Japan to the Catholic Faith, it can hardly be argued that Father Ho Lung has an aversion to the bringing of the Gospel to non-Christian cultures. Equally important, however, is the fact that Father Ho Lung's great Jesuit forebear could also be considered the patron saint of inculturation. As Robert Schreiter notes in "The Legacy of St. Francis Xavier: Inculturation of the Gospel Then and Now":

> Notable about Xavier was his commitment to learning languages. He realized that without being able to communicate with people in their own medium, the effectiveness of his preaching would be much diminished. As imperfectly as he managed to achieve proficiency, he recognized the necessity of striving to speak in the language of the people whom he was addressing.[3]

Father Ho Lung is following faithfully in the footsteps of his favorite saint. His primary language is the universal language of love, shining forth in his work for the poorest of the poor, but another language that he has always used is the universal language of music. Like St. Francis Xavier, he recognizes "the necessity of striving to speak in the language of the people whom he [is] addressing" and has learned "to communicate with people in their own medium," which in the case of the people of the Jamaican ghettos is the medium of traditional Caribbean music and rhythm.

If music be the food of love, as Shakespeare maintained, Father Ho Lung has fed the poor of Jamaica with a charitable feast.

---

3. *East Asian Pastoral Review*, Volume 44 (2007), Number 1.

Chapter Four

··

REGGAE PRIEST

FATHER Ho Lung's fidelity to the Magisterium of the Church manifested itself in an article in a Jamaican newspaper in September 1971, just a couple of months after his ordination.[1] The article defended the Church against the anti-Catholic bigotry and propaganda of a militant Protestant sect. The Florida-based sect, known as Laymen for Religious Liberty, was staging a program of talks at the Oceana Hotel, entitled "In Search of Anti-Christ," the advertising materials for which displayed a prominent photograph of the pope at that time, Paul VI.

"What," asked the newly ordained priest, "are we to infer from this title when juxtaposed with a picture of the head of the Catholic Church? What can we surmise to be the 'truth' that will be told about Catholic Jesuits, the title of the second day's talks?" Concluding that it could be safely inferred that the purpose of the talks would be to attack the Catholic Church scurrilously, Father Ho Lung proceeded with a spirited defense of the Church in general and the Church's role in Jamaica in particular:

----

1. *Daily Gleaner*, September 7, 1971.

There are 180,000 Roman Catholics in this island: rich people, poor people, from the good and generous Issa family to the humble Miss Pansy, basic school teacher in Mona Common. Sir Alexander Bustamante was a Catholic. Marcus Garvey died a Catholic. Claude McKay, the poet, Roger Mais, the novelist, were Catholics. Many other prominent members of our society are Catholics. Over 65,000 students in this island are being educated mostly by Roman Catholics.

Playing the role of investigative journalist, Father Ho Lung phoned the Laymen for Religious Liberty, and was told that the group intended to attack "the hierarchy of the Catholic Church," leading him to defend the hierarchical character of the Church against her detractors:

The Catholic Church is a hierarchical church. And attacking the hierarchy means not only attacking our head, it means attacking Jamaican Archbishop Samuel Carter. It also means attacking Sr. Benedict, Sr. Maureen Clare, Sr. Martin, Deacon Ronald Thwaites, Fr. Alfred Lee, myself, and the many others who are part of the hierarchy of the Catholic Church.

And yes, we are engaged in the works for which the group says we should be given credit: we run orphanages, homes for the destitute, trade training centres, schools, hospitals, but as Mother Teresa states, we are not social workers. You cannot separate our works from who we are. We are part of the hierarchy of the Catholic Church, and our intention it to be of use to our people and to bring Christ to them, to build up the kingdom of God. . . .

> I do not believe it is good for these visitors to come into our island and stir up controversy, create confusion, and foment division. Christ himself preached the good news, not a message of hatred and disunity and divisiveness. I do not see the good news being preached by this group of visitors.

This broadside against sectarianism marked the newly ordained priest's public debut. It was his baptism of fire into the culture wars that were ripping twentieth century society apart. It also illustrated certain attributes that would become a hallmark of his future ministry: the willingness to speak out publicly and defiantly against injustice, the love for Jamaica and its people, a love for the poor, and, above all, a love for Christ. It also highlighted the influence of Mother Teresa on the young priest's development. He understood, as did she, that Catholics who give themselves in service to the poor are not merely social workers. They are not motivated primarily by the desire to make people more comfortable physically but by the desire to serve Jesus in His presence among them. The Catholic missionary sees Jesus in the emaciated faces of the poor, and wants the poor to see Jesus in the faces of those who are helping them. As Mother Teresa said to US Senator Sam Brownback: "All for Jesus. All for Jesus. All for Jesus. All for Jesus."[2]

Like Mother Teresa, Father Ho Lung would offer *all for Jesus* in a life of service to the poor. Such service would, however, lead him in surprising directions and find him in the most unexpected places. In 1973 it found him near the top of the record charts as the recording of one of his own songs, *Sinner*, by "Father Ho Lung and Friends" became a surprise hit

2. Senator Sam Brownback, *From Power to Purpose*, Nashville, TN: Thomas Nelson, 2007, p. 69.

single. One of Jamaica's main newspapers, the *Daily Gleaner*, voiced the surprise of everyone at the emergence of the Reggae Priest: "A 34-year-old Roman Catholic priest . . . and lecturer in the Literature department at UWI [University of the West Indies] . . . is, believe it or not, the island's newest Reggae recording sensation." The priest's single was "one of the most requested and fast selling records in town."[3]

The *Gleaner* reported that Father Ho Lung had written "Sinner" as a riposte to Ernie Smith's "Life is Just for Living." This was confirmed many years later in Father Ho Lung's memories of his motivation for writing the song. "I was simply amazed at the discrepancies between the rich and the poor, and the lack of sensitivity on the part of those who had the means of helping to alleviate the situation. Ernie Smith had a song on the charts at that time called 'Life is Just for Living,' which I considered hedonistic and morally destructive to the island. I thought it needed to be countered so I wrote 'Sinner.'"[4]

The lyrics of *Sinner* are a direct riposte to the lyrics of Smith's hit record:

> Sinner you're going to hell.
> Master, you've taken leave of yourself.
> Man, you're good as dead,
> Sitting in the sunshine,
> Bathing in your wealth
> Watching all the sufferers in hell . . .
> Brother, please hear my plea,
> You can help,
> O can't you see,
> Can't you see?
> Man, you could be free,

---

3. *Daily Gleaner*, October 10, 1973.
4. Brother Arnold, unpublished manuscript.

Working in the sunshine,
Freeing up your wealth,
Helping all the sufferers in hell.

As *Sinner* was shooting up the charts, a curious reporter from the *Daily Gleaner* interviewed the young priest who had become the talk of the town. The photograph that accompanied the published article shows a young, broadly smiling priest, in clerical garb, hands in pockets, with shoulder length hair cascading down from beneath a trendy hat. He arrived at the recording studio carrying a pear and sandwiches and spoke readily to the reporter of the philosophy that had inspired the hit song: "In Jamaica you have people who are very poor, and others who are the opposite. Although not all rich people are oppressors, some don't really care, like employers who give their employees very little wages."[5] He explained that "Father Ho Lung and Friends" consisted of around ten people who had got together to record an album, "Bread and Wine," a year or so earlier. "Sinner" and the planned follow-up single "Babylon a Catch Me" were taken from the new album, *Jasmine and Jeremiah.* He also told the reporter that his priestly duties prevented him from making live appearances and that all profits from the recordings went to the work of the Church.

A month or so later, on November 18, "Sinner" had risen to number three on the Jamaican charts, its highest position. Marvin Gaye held the top slot and Father Ho Lung's single was selling better than other American artists on the charts in the same week, including Smokey Robinson, the Manhattans, the Chi-Lites, the Eagles, and Al Green. He was also higher in the charts than the giants of the Jamaican pop scene, including Bob Marley, Dennis Brown, Peter Tosh, and the Maytals. In

---

5. *Daily Gleaner*, October 10, 1973

the same week, the *Jamaican Daily News* carried the headline
"Father Ho Lung Does *Not* Sing Sinner," quoting a "distressed"
Father Ho Lung who was at pains to make it plain that the
vocals on the track were actually sung by a singer named Danny
Harrison, whom the newspaper sensationally and erroneously
claimed was "a cousin of the ex-Beatle George Harrison."[6] He
was, in fact, an unknown Canadian singer who had married a
Jamaican, was living on the island, and had just happened to be
hanging around the studio when Father Ho Lung and Friends
were recording "Sinner." "He walked through the studio while
we were working on the track, and asked if he could try the
vocal," Ho Lung explained. "He tried it and then we tried other
singers afterwards. We felt that his was a perfect fit. It's sort of
an anomaly."[7] Harrison's growling Canadian accent accompanied by the Caribbean rhythm was certainly anomalous, creating an odd cross-fertilization between American country music
and Jamaican reggae, as though Johnny Cash had collaborated
with Bob Marley. It worked well and it is little surprise, in hindsight, that the record proved such a success.

It was, however, a huge surprise to everyone involved at the
time. Father Ho Lung explained that the record was made as a
fundraising venture for a newly formed interracial charity, the
Brotherhood of Man, of which he was chairman. Founded to
promote racial harmony in Jamaica, its purpose was to show
that people of all races could unite to alleviate the island's social
problems. It was hoped that any money raised from sales of
the record would be used to provide care for abandoned children and to help find foster homes for them. With this greater
vision in mind, the disparate elements that came together to

<hr>

6. *Jamaican Daily News*, November 18, 1973.
7. Father Ho Lung, interview with the author.

make *Sinner* such a success serve as a metaphor for the vision itself: an ethnically Chinese priest writes a reggae song about social problems which is sung by a Caucasian Canadian immigrant, married to a native Jamaican. The song was itself the very incarnation of interracial harmony!

Unfortunately, the media had dubbed Father Ho Lung the "singing priest," leading many to the understandable conclusion that he was the vocalist on the track. Anyone who compared the rasping aggression of Harrison's vocals with the sing-song softness of the priest's gentle Jamaican lilt would have realized instantly that Father Ho Lung could not have been the vocalist. Nonetheless, the general assumption was that he had been the vocalist and he was determined to dispel the myth. He told the reporter from the *Jamaican Daily News* that because *Sinner* was a fundraising venture and nobody involved expected it to be such a howling success, credits were not considered terribly important. It was agreed that the record should be released with credits reading simply "Father Ho Lung and Friends" and that this had been the source of the subsequent confusion. The reporter described Father Ho Lung as "stunned" by the record's success. "Nobody expected it to take off," he told her. "It is a complete shock. We only expected it to sell 500 or so."

It is tempting to draw parallels between Father Ho Lung, the "singing priest," and Sister Luc Gabriel, the "singing nun," who shot to worldwide fame in 1963, ten years earlier, with her international hit single, *Dominique*, which made number one on the Billboard Hot 100 in the United States. Like Elvis Presley and a host of other top stars, the Belgian nun appeared on the *Ed Sullivan Show*, a sure sign of success. Her appearance on the show, in January 1964, was only a few weeks before the Beatles made their first live television appearance in the USA on the same show. It is also tempting to draw parallels with Sister Janet

Mead, an Australian nun who had a hit record in 1974 with her rock version of the Lord's Prayer. Like Father Ho Lung, Sister Janet also made number three in her own nation's chart but, unlike Father Ho Lung, she also scored a huge hit in the United States, reaching number four on the Billboard Hot 100.

Tragically, however, neither of the "singing nuns" dealt very well with their worldly success. Sister Luc Gabriel left the convent in 1967 and soon adopted a negative attitude toward the Catholic Church, becoming an outspoken advocate of sexual "liberation" and contraception. She also adopted a homosexual lifestyle. Within months of leaving the convent, under her new stage-name of Luc Dominique, she recorded a song called "Glory Be to God for the Golden Pill," which was a commercial failure. In spite of many attempts to revitalize her recording career, she never managed to emulate the success of her one big hit. In the late 1970s she was prosecuted by the Belgian government for tax evasion. Citing their financial difficulties in a note, she and her "partner" Annie Pécher chose the final solution of despair and committed suicide by overdosing on barbiturates and alcohol in 1985.

The other "singing nun," Sister Janet Mead, has fared much better, although she describes the record's success as a "horrible time" in her life, citing her worldwide celebrity as creating pressures that led her to question her faith. She survived the experience of fame, largely by shying away from it. Today she is still an active Catholic and is involved in the Romero Community, which is described as a "conservative charismatic religious movement." She now works with the poorest of the poor, "assisting aged care, destitute men and women, refugees and the oppressed in Australian society and beyond." It is gratifying to see that Sister Janet's path has converged with that of Father Ho Lung, not least because, like Father Ho Lung, she donated all the profits from her hit records to charity. The final sentence of the short biography on Sister Janet's *MySpace* page serves as a summary and summation of her musical legacy: "As a woman who had it all, gave it away and continued to be very committed to equality and social justice, she leaves many in the fickle music industry of today something to admire."

Father Ho Lung's sudden fame did not tempt him to take the path of worldliness and despair, which engulfed and finally consumed Sister Luc Gabriel, neither was his faith threatened by his experience as had been the case with Sister Janet Mead. "When *Sinner* really took off, I ran away. I said to myself, I don't think I want that much to do with this. I was worried about fame and glory. I was worried about pride and getting caught up in the pop world. I just didn't want to go in that direction. I pulled back from it. But it had made its point, thank God. It had made its point, and became very, very popular." Although Father Ho Lung declined when the recording company offered him a record deal, the experience of success had given him the incentive to keep on writing songs. Flushed with this newfound confidence and enthusiasm, he wrote some of his most enduring and popular songs at this time, such as *Enter into Jerusalem*, in which the anger that had animated *Sinner* is replaced with the joyful inclusiveness of a life in Christ. He recalls that most people in the music industry and in the wider establishment were accepting of him. "People were delighted frankly. Overall, I think the music industry found it moving, and they were able to identify with a religious man, a Catholic priest, on that level. I was wary, I was watchful, but I could see that it was doing its work; the rich were hearing." There was, however, a darker and threatening side to the success. As *Sinner* was riding high in the charts, Father Ho Lung received a death threat. "I received a telephone call from a man. He didn't identify who he was, but he said that he planned to kill me." The unidentified caller claimed that he planned to shoot the priest the next time he went to the airport. Father Ho Lung shrugged the threat aside and was even encouraged that his hit song had clearly made a real impact. "It confirmed that something had struck home. The message, clearly, was right and needed to be heard."

For the reggae priest, the music could never be separated from the message. Indeed, it was a servant to the message. The message was a call for repentance and renewal, and for the bad news of injustice to make way for the good news of the Gospel. Like his Master, Father Ho Lung came to bring good news to the poor. "He moves and creates in total solidarity with the teeming poor of the slums and the ghettoes," says Brother Arnold. "His music throbs with their pain, grief, hunger—yes with their hopes and fears and sometimes ecstasy. He is a Jesuit with about 10 years of university under his belt yet he speaks the language of the streets and 'yards' both in his lyrics and his toe tapping rhythms."[8] Ultimately Father Ho Lung is the reggae priest because, first and foremost, he is a priest of the ghetto.

8.   Brother Arnold, unpublished manuscript.

Chapter Five

·······························

GHETTO PRIEST

FATHER Ho Lung's new-found fame presented him with a platform to preach. As an unknown, newly-ordained priest, his words had only reached the small circle of people with whom he worked and prayed. Now, as the celebrated "reggae priest," it seemed that the whole of Jamaica was listening.

In January 1974, as his hit single, *Sinner*, was still riding high in the charts, a Jamaican newspaper published an extensive interview, describing Ho Lung as "perhaps the greatest enigma to emerge in the entertainment spotlight [because] the young man whose lyrics and music come pounding from every juke box, radio and discotheque is actually a Roman Catholic priest." The journalist emphasized that this paradoxical melding of the priest and the pop singer helped to explain the social consciousness of the record's lyrics:

> *Sinner* ... is infused with a relevance rarely encountered in locally produced records. Wrapped around a snappy and infectious reggae beat, the song is peopled with realities from several strata of contemporary Jamaican society: the sufferer, the oppressor, the girl heavy with a baby, the labourer digging at a rock.[1]

—————

1. Unknown Jamaican newspaper, January 1974.

Asked by the interviewer why a priest writes pop music, Father Ho Lung responded that it was all about preaching the Gospel: "The more involved I get in this type of music, the deeper my conviction that reggae and soul music provide a most powerful medium for communicating with young people."

At around the same time, Father Ho Lung's words from the pulpit were also making the headlines. "Politicians Set Youths a Bad Example—Ho Lung" was the headline in the *Jamaica Daily News* on January 25, and the *Daily Gleaner* on the following day highlighted his keynote address to two thousand young people at the annual gathering of Methodist youth. The fact that the organizers selected him as the keynote speaker was further indication that the success of the hit record had given him a platform from which to preach.

As Father Ho Lung recalled those heady days when his hit record was near the top of the charts, I asked him what his fellow Jesuits thought of the whole strange scenario. On the one hand, he was a lecturer in literature at the University of the West Indies and rector of the Aquinas Centre at Mona, and yet, on the other, he was a successful pop star. I was mindful of the supercilious response of the academic establishment at Oxford to J. R. R. Tolkien and C. S. Lewis, both Oxford dons, after their respective success with bestselling novels. When Lewis and Tolkien became famous for writing their books, they faced a great deal of snobbery and a degree of elitist sneering from their academic colleagues for condescending to the level of popular culture. I wondered whether Father Ho Lung's Jesuit colleagues were similarly unsympathetic and aloof, or whether they thought him an amusing and amiable eccentric. Confirming that there were "strong undercurrents of resentment and anger," he sought to put the matter in perspective, drawing on the wisdom of hindsight:

I think it all seemed a little odd to them. I had begun musicals with the kids, and I was writing music also for the liturgy, and I used to take kids to the slum yards and have them work two or three times a week with these very, very poor people. I was not spending all my time at the school, but was spending increasing amounts of time with the poor. The Jesuits were good men, don't get me wrong, but I was quite rebellious at that time. I felt that the changes in Jesuit education weren't making sense, and I made it very clear to my colleagues that the school didn't have a soul, it didn't have a clear purpose. It tended to be all about academics and football, rather than anything else, anything spiritual or formative. I think my fellow Jesuits saw my actions and my motives in that light. Mind you, I must also admit that I was fairly careless about classes. I guess part of it would have been lack of motivation. I think that I deserved to be chastised and to be, in a sense, looked at as somebody who was irresponsible.

Although the reggae priest was also a self-confessed rebel priest, his labors continued to bear good fruit. In September 1975, his musical, *Brother Soul, Sister Song*, opened to rave reviews. "The music, the singing, and the sheer enthusiasm and sincerity of the four very talented young performers in the cast are so disarming," wrote the reviewer in the *Daily Gleaner*, "that by the time the third song is finished, whether you like it or not, you like it."[2] The reviewer also encapsulated the infectious charm of Father Ho Lung's music, which is one of the secrets of its enduring success:

---

2. *Daily Gleaner*, September 13, 1975.

> The thing about Father Ho Lung's music is that it
> is so derivative of so many different types of music
> that each song, on hearing it for the first time,
> becomes immediately familiar. One feels one has
> heard it before, and it has the instant impact of
> an old standard, in that one is delighted to hear it
> "again," for the first time.
>
> This is not to say that any one of his songs is
> directly imitative of other songs; Ho Lung's gift, as
> a songwriter, is that he is able to capture the quint-
> essential attributes of any particular style of music
> and infuse his songs with them. Then, within the
> format of any of these given styles he places his lyr-
> ics, his message. His sermons.

The reviewer also emphasized the liberal and catholic use
of different musical styles employed in *Brother Soul, Sister
Song*: "Its geography covers everything from Trench Town to
Motown, from Broadway to Nashville, from the Deep South
of America to the North Country of England. There are the
sounds of dub and reggae, Country and Western, gospel, spiritual, soul, mento, rock, jazz, blues. There are ballads, show
tunes, folk songs, madrigals, even a hymn or two."

Having waxed eloquently on the intrinsic qualities of Father
Ho Lung's muse, the reviewer descended to the level of banal
modernism in his sideswipe at the perceived Puritanism of
the Vatican. "There was a time," the reviewer pontificated,
"when the very thought of a Jesuit going into show business
would have thrown the Vatican into an uproar of outrage. But
times change, thank God, and the Church in recent years has
begun to change along with them." As with most modern-
ists, the reviewer is ignorant of history. If he had a modicum
of historical knowledge he would have known that Catholic

priests have composed popular music throughout the centuries without the Vatican being thrown into apoplexy. The famous priest-composer Vivaldi springs instantly to mind. Others include Thoinot Arbeau, best known for his *Orchésographie*, a study of late sixteenth-century Renaissance social dance, and for his composition of the jaunty Christmas carol, "Ding Dong Merrily On High." Far from the Vatican being thrown into "an uproar of outrage" by its priest composers, it has even been known to canonize them, as was the case with the Jesuit, Jean de Brébeuf, composer of another Christmas carol, "Twas in the Moon of Wintertime," also known as the Huron Carol. In the field of literature, the Jesuit martyr-saints Edmund Campion and Robert Southwell wrote plays and popular poetry, and the great St. John of the Cross composed some of the finest metaphysical poetry ever written. There is, of course, a huge difference between the composition of popular music and literature, on the one hand, and "show business," on the other. Since "show business" is all about *show*, i.e. fame, and *business*, i.e., fortune, it is true that the Vatican would frown upon any of its priests pursuing such a meretricious profession. Since, however, Father Ho Lung has never written his music for either fame or fortune but, on the contrary, has always donated all profits from his music to the poor, it can be stated definitively that he has never been in "show business," in the sense in which that tawdry phrase is normally used. Indeed, and as we have seen in the wake of the success of *Sinner*, he has always shied away from "show business" whenever he felt its corrupting presence encroaching upon his vocation to the priesthood.

In spite of the good reviews, *Brother Soul, Sister Song* caused a degree of controversy due to its criticism of the government. One of the songs in the show, *God and Caesar*, was banned by the Jamaican Broadcasting Corporation when it was released as a single. The song was initially inspired by Father Ho Lung's appearance on a TV panel show with other clergymen, in which he took the minority view that churchmen should not necessarily comply with everything the government says.[3] His view, however unpopular at the time, has clearly been vindicated in the wake of the rise of secular fundamentalism and its attempts to outlaw Christian morality from public life; and it has also been vindicated by many of the great saints of history, each of whom defied the tyranny of secularism, such as St. Thomas Becket, St. Thomas More and St. Maximilian Kolbe, to name but a few of the most obvious. Ultimately, of course, and as the title of *God and Caesar* suggests, Father Ho Lung was taking Christ Himself as his model. As Christ's own example teaches, Christians cannot render unto Caesar the things that are God's.

While writing popular music for the stage, Father Ho Lung continued to write music for the liturgy. This was proving equally controversial. In May 1976, the Jamaican Catholic newspaper, *Catholic Opinion*, voiced the views of those who were affronted by the Caribbean rhythms of liturgical songs, such as "Enter into Jerusalem," as well as those who leapt to their defense. In the latter camp was Sister Clare Marie Figueroa, a Franciscan who also taught at a primary school in Kingston: "The hymn 'Enter into Jerusalem' is a rhythmic, stirring invitation to worship and praise God, not unlike the psalm of which it is an echo. The majestic impelling invitation of: 'Enter into Jerusalem—Let us go to God's house' is reinforced by the colloquial, 'We go celebrate, O Israel,' because this line imitates exactly the idiom of the speaker whose ecstasy is there unmistakably." Sister Clare Marie then invited those other correspondents who had raised the controversy over Father Ho Lung's

---

3. *Catholic Register* [Toronto, Canada], May 7, 1977.

music "to hear the fifth and sixth graders at St. Anne's Primary School sing this with genuine participation," promising that her students' "joy and sincerity should be convincing."[4]

In an interview given in late 1977, Father Ho Lung described the way in which he composed his music. Much of it came to him quickly, sometimes in dreams, after which he had complete recall, and sometimes when he was meditating. He never produced music on demand but the inspiration flowed freely when he was alone and in a quiet place. He revealed that most of the songs on one of his albums had been revealed to him while he was on a two-day spiritual retreat. "I didn't even have any paper with me, or anything to write with, so I was a bit worried that I would not remember everything when I got back, but I did, and it all turned out well."[5]

While the celebrity and controversy surrounding the musical activities of the reggae priest captured the headlines, the ghetto priest continued with his work for the poor, a labor of love which went largely unnoticed by the wider world. Continuing to lecture at the University of the West Indies, he developed a pastoral ministry in the nearby slum area of Mona Common. In 1975 his deep involvement with the poor and their affliction came to the fore in a confrontation with Jamaica's Minister of Housing, Tony Spaulding. On hearing of Spaulding's plans to demolish the shacks in the slum neighborhood of Rema, Father Ho Lung mobilized the public and instructed the people to form a human barricade in the way of the bulldozers. Faced with such resolute resistance, the government was forced to delay the demolition of the slums.

In July 1976, Father Ho Lung shocked those in attendance

4. *Catholic Opinion*, May 28, 1976.
5. Unidentified and undated Jamaican newspaper review of Fr. Ho Lung and Friends' fourth album [late 1977].

at a Valedictory Service for graduating seniors at a high school
in Port Antonio when he warned them of the dangers of putting their trust in politicians. "At this time our island is shot
through with falsehood at all levels," he told the graduating
class. "We should not depend on our politicians."[6] He also
admonished the students to use the gifts of their education to
help others less fortunate, urging them to give as Christ had
given of Himself.

In April 1977, Father Ho Lung and Friends played twenty-
seven concerts in Canada, sponsored by Air Jamaica, the first
of many trips to North America over the following years. In
July the group played a series of concerts, featuring songs from
the soon-to-be-released fourth album. As always, the concerts
were held to raise money for the poor, in this case to assist
Father Ho Lung's ministry to the homeless, including those
displaced by the destruction of the Rema slums. Three years
earlier, Father Ho Lung had formed a Catholic co-operative for
the poor sponsored by the Church, which gave fifty cents for
every dollar collected. The co-op grew peanuts and vegetables,
and raised goats, chickens, and rabbits. The women sewed,
knitted, and crocheted. The co-op eventually raised enough
funds to re-house some fifty families (approximately 180 people). Furthermore, with the help of the Canadian University
Services Overseas (CUSO), Father Ho Lung built a basic school
which also provided medical services in the area of the slums.

Father Ho Lung's founding of the co-operative signified his
loyalty and adherence to the authentic social teaching of the
Church as distinct from the pseudo-marxism of the liberation theology that John Paul II would so vigorously condemn
a few years later. The Church's social teaching as defined in

---

6. *Daily Gleaner*, July 24, 1976.

papal encyclicals, such as *Rerum novarum* by Leo XIII (1891) or *Quadragesimo anno* by Pius XI (1931), and more recently by John Paul II in *Centessimus annus* (1991) and Benedict XVI in *Caritas in veritate* (2009), enshrines the family at the heart of socio-economic life and calls for subsidiarity as the economic and political means by which the family's sacrosanct place is to be nurtured and preserved. In opposition to the Big Business of corporate globalism and the Big Government of welfare-state socialism, subsidiarity necessitates the promotion of small businesses and producers' cooperatives as a means of providing the workforce with true independence from wage-slavery or welfare-dependency. This principle was encapsulated by Pope Leo XIII in *Rerum novarum*:

> The law, therefore, should favour ownership and its policy should be to induce as many people as possible to become owners. Many excellent results will follow from this; and first of all, property will certainly become more equitably divided. . . . If working people can be encouraged to look forward to obtaining a share in the land, the result will be that the gulf between vast wealth and deep poverty will be bridged over, and the two orders will be brought nearer together.[7]

Inspired by the Church's social teaching, a Catholic priest in the Mondragon region of Spain's Basque Country, Father José María Arizmendi (1915–1976), had founded a network of cooperatives in the 1940s, which was destined to transform the beleaguered and poverty-stricken region. Whereas the Mondragon experiment, as it is sometimes called, is perhaps the most dramatic example of the practical and successful

---

7. Leo XIII, *Rerum Novarum*, 46-47.

application of the Church's social teaching, Father Ho Lung, in his own modest way, was practicing exactly the same principles with the founding of the agricultural co-operative in the midst of the Kingston ghetto. In helping the poor to establish the co-operative, he was putting the pope's teaching into practice, inducing "as many people as possible to become owners" and encouraging the poor of the ghetto "to look forward to obtaining a share in the land."

Father Ho Lung's advocacy of another aspect of subsidiarity was evident during a concert tour of Trinidad and Tobago in January 1978, when he told a journalist that he wished to preserve the local indigenous cultures of the Caribbean: "He stresses that, though in the Caribbean we have many things in common, we must not tend to standardize our culture because standardization destroys the differences which manifest the genius of our Caribbean peoples."[8] In seeking to champion and preserve the beautiful diversity of the various Caribbean cultures in the face of globalist standardization, the Jamaican priest was echoing the words of the great English writer, G. K. Chesterton, who warned that "the coming peril" to all cultures was "vulgarity" or "the danger of standardization by a low standard."[9]

On Christmas Day 1977, a few days before their departure for the tour of Trinidad and Tobago, Father Ho Lung and Friends reached by far its largest and widest audience when the BBC broadcast their performance, via satellite, to seven countries around the world, reaching a potential audience of one billion

---

8. *Catholic News*, January 22, 1978.
9. G. K. Chesterton, *Culture and the Coming Peril*, London: University of London, p. 18.

people.[10] It was all a far cry from the ghetto and yet, for the ghetto priest, the music was always at the service of the poor.

Father Ho Lung's fight for the poor continued as he opened the eyes of the public to the deplorable conditions at the Eventide Home, a public alms house at which more rats were in residence than people. Conditions were unspeakably horrific. Residents were living in their own feces and urine, some were dying of malnutrition, and others were literally being eaten alive by the rats.

> "In my part-time voluntary work at Eventide, I met the poorest of people anyone could find on the face of the earth," recalls Fr. Ho Lung. "It was here that I saw a little boy, David, tied with cloth improvised as ropes to an iron chair. He was about seven years old. He lived in this almshouse where seven hundred people were literally dumped rather than cared for by the government. The poor little boy had been in the hot blazing summer sun since six that morning. It was 1pm at the time of my visit.
>
> "David had on just a brief. He was sweating and was dazed in the heat. Flies had pitched on the faeces that he had passed and which was scattered on the ground about him. I approached David with the intention of untying him and cleaning him. But his tiny bowl of rice had fallen into his mess and he was picking out the rice grains and eating it. I was angry, and confronted the workers. They explained that he was a troublesome child who grabbed everything including other's food and created confusion. They said they could not bother with him. The workers

10. As reported in the *Trinidad Guardian*, January 5, 1978, and in the *Jamaican Gleaner*, January 8, 1978.

laughed when I loosened the cloth that bound his
hands and took him to a bathing pan."[11]

Two young men, Hayden Augustine and Brian Kerr, who
shared Father Ho Lung's vision of giving themselves freely in
service to the poor, accompanied Father Ho Lung on this horrific visit to Eventide. Ho Lung described the heinous scene
when the three men returned the next day to visit David.

> "In the night, we heard he was attacked by rats, his
> lips and ear lobes were bitten and he seemed to have
> died of a heart attack. We went to the dormitory and
> uncovered the bed sheet from the body and simply
> wept when we saw him. Old ladies and old men had
> also been bitten by rats; women's breasts, men's and
> women's lips, ears, and necks. The entire place was
> a garbage dump of wasted and rejected humanity.
> This is where Christ would have gone if He visited
> Jamaica today. These would be His people and He
> would be their God. He would not be out just giving
> talks about poverty. We left the grounds of Eventide
> and went home to pray. All night I wrestled with
> the Lord, tormented by His calling, besieged by His
> presence."[12]

In this agony in the garden of his own soul, Father Ho Lung
battled with the enormity of the problem of poverty. Surely
it was simply impossible to do anything to help. He felt the
dreadfulness of the situation and fought with his own feelings
of futility. The huge problem of poverty seemed insoluble. How
could he, a simple priest, take care of the poor? He had nothing but his two Masters degrees and his doctorate. The Lord

---

11. Brother Arnold, unpublished manuscript.
12. Ibid.

seemed to be saying that he had to give everything up, even the Jesuit community, and walk in the footsteps of Jesus, His Beloved Son. "I was in torture. I wept and I prayed all night. Next day I felt washed and purified by the struggle with my God. I capitulated. 'Whatever You will, my Lord,' I said."[13]

Father Ho Lung shared his mystical experience with Hayden and Brian. They reflected on the situation and understood that the only way to begin work with the poor was to be with them in their most dreadful suffering. They must embrace the suffering of the poorest of their brothers and sisters.

A few months later, on May 20, 1980, tragedy struck the residents of Eventide when a fire swept through one of the wards, engulfing the old and dilapidated wooden building. It was razed to the ground, leaving only zinc sheets, ashes and the charred remains of most of the ward's residents. Over 150 elderly women died, making it the deadliest fire in Jamaican history. Father Ho Lung, adopting the local dialect, recalls how one of the few survivors described the nightmare in which she found herself: "It was the blackest of nights when the fire circled the bottom floor and rose up in a high blaze to trap and swallow up all the people. Nobody knows what was going on. It was sudden. Then the screams. If you ever see how people ran like mad ants, and we fall on each other. I jump out of bed and cough till I nearly dead."[14] The government was forced to eat humble pie and the prime minister, Michael Manley, declared a national day of mourning on the day that the victims were laid to rest in a mass grave.

The unprecedented disaster prompted two reggae artists, Yellowman and General Echo, to record songs about the

---

13. Ibid.
14. Quoted in Payne, op. cit., pp. 20–21.

tragedy, both of which were hits, but Father Ho Lung was moving beyond the protest song and the pulpit-preaching to a practical and loving engagement with his nation's poor.

> I felt that everything that I had done up until that
> time had been somehow hypocritical. I was preach-
> ing the word of God but not really living it. I was
> aware of the degradation of the poor in my own
> island community. I knew I was not as serious about
> the poor as I should be, and that meant that I was
> not as serious about Christ as I should be.
>
> Certainly I was destined only to condemnation.
> Revelations 3:16 haunted me, *Because you are luke-
> warm, and neither cold nor hot, I will spew you out of
> my mouth.* Supposedly, as a priest and a Christian,
> I had sacrificed my life for Jesus totally. But I was a
> hypocrite. No self-sacrificing priest was I, though I
> stood daily at the Altar of Sacrifice and presided over
> the sacrificial death of the Lord Jesus in identifica-
> tion with Him. He had given His Life to me. Daily I
> experienced His love, such warm consolation, such
> lovely intimacy, and a wonderful call to be united
> with Him and the Heavenly Father. But I did not
> love Him enough, not His Cross, which every adult
> must embrace fully, if we truly love Christ.[15]

Father Ho Lung had reached a defining moment in his life, a
moment that would radically change the way that he lived and
the way that he loved. Henceforth the ghetto priest would live
the life of the Cross in brotherhood with the poor. A life of joyful service with Christ on the Cross was beginning.

---

15. Brother Arnold, unpublished manuscript.

Chapter Six

....

A BAND OF BROTHERS

We few, we happy few, we band of brothers ...
—William Shakespeare
(*Henry V*, Act IV, Scene 3)

IT IS OFTEN said that life begins at forty. Whether this is always true, it could certainly be said to be true of the life of Father Ho Lung. He had achieved much in his first forty years of life. From humble beginnings as the child of impoverished immigrants, he had attained two Masters degrees and a doctorate. He had been ordained to the Jesuit priesthood and had taught at Boston College, as well as at the University of the West Indies. As if this were not enough to cause the poor man's son to rest on his laurels, he had also had a number of hit records and had performed on television, via satellite, to an international audience of millions. And yet, as the priest reached his fortieth year, all of this seemed as nothing, as "a chronicle of wasted time" in which his "dear time's waste" was but "the expense of spirit in a waste of shame."[1] The suffering of the rejected and the abandoned did not permit him to be content with a mere

---

1. From Shakespeare's sonnets 106, 30 and 129 respectively. The ascent to Shakespearean grandiloquence does not seem indecorous considering Father Ho Lung's doctorate in literature and his professorship at UWI.

academic career. He felt a compulsion to lay aside the creature comforts and to take up the Cross of Christ:

> The Cross specifically meant giving up my two masters' degrees, my doctorate, and a life of the intellect: that meant casting aside years of studies and not only that but my Jesuit Community, the largest and the most powerful male Religious Order in the Church. The thought of losing all that terrified me. But poverty and injustices had spread like cancer in the lives of our poor and indeed the entire lives of the ghetto people. I had to do something or die spiritually. The island's violence, drugs, hunger, prostitution and the threat of communism haunted me day and night in the 1970's. Despair filled me and a sense of bitterness that neither politics, nor the rich, nor the Christian faith was giving enough attention to these problems. I had to do something. I had to start somewhere, do something specific. To change social structures was literally impossible. I gave many public talks about social justice and preached the same from the pulpit. I taught at local and foreign universities. It all seemed empty. Not for a second do I regret giving up the scholastics or not going after material comforts. I have no doubt; I made the right choice, for the Lord, for the Church and for the Poor.[2]

The "right choice" was the decision to leave the community of the Jesuits and to found, with a handful of like-minded friends, the Brothers of the Poor.

Let's look at the months leading up to the making of that crucial choice, months that the skeptic or the psychologist

---

2. Brother Arnold, unpublished manuscript.

might consider a mid-life crisis but which served as the catalyst for the change of life and the conversion of spirit.

In June 1980, Father Ho Lung flew to Canada to seek support for the still flourishing agricultural co-op which he had founded several years earlier. "Jamaica," he told a Canadian reporter, "is a great big wounded animal. It's torn by confusion and suffering. It's an angry island. But at the same time it is absolutely beautiful. The island shows the power of God in its mountains and sea, and the nature of the people shows God's generosity and kindness."[3] Sharing the anger and wounds of his fellow countrymen, the disgruntled Jesuit never forgot that he and they were also greatly blessed. "We are a strong, spiritual people," he told a Jamaican reporter several months later, "with strong feelings, love of laughter and music, and we have an inherent childlikeness all evolving in a central culture."[4] When this reporter told him that he is known to most Jamaicans as the "Radical Priest," he responded negatively. "No," he insisted, "I'm the practicing priest. I like to practice what I preach." For all his rhetoric and all his outspokenness, Father Ho Lung was never pursuing a political or ideological agenda. He was simply trying to be a good disciple of Christ.

At the end of 1980, Father Ho Lung and Friends released a new single, *Christmas Mento*, and produced a new show, *The Sound of Christmas*. Hayden Augustine, one of the small group of young men who were working with Father Ho Lung in his ministry to the poor, recalled the violence of the time and the fearlessness with which Father Ho Lung dealt with the imminent danger in which they found themselves. "It was violent in those days, before the elections of October 1980, but Father was

---

3. *New Times*, June 22, 1980.
4. Unidentified newspaper cutting, December 19, 1980.

unfazed. We were going through the bullets, going through the roadblocks. I thought that there's something wrong with this man. This man is crazy!"

During 1981 Father Ho Lung's relationship with the Jesuits, which had been strained for some time, reached a breaking point. In July, he was granted a leave of absence by his Jesuit Superiors. He and his group of young students spent the month in the hills of Newcastle in intense prayer and discernment, the result of which was the decision to found the Brothers of the Poor (the community would not adopt the name "Missionaries of the Poor" until 1992). Two years later, on August 1, 1983, fully resolved to pursue the new path of radical poverty, Father Ho Lung formally petitioned for an indult of secularization, *Praevio Experimento*, which would be granted on December 5, 1983, by the Sacred Congregation for Religious. In 1989 Fr. Ho Lung would be formally incardinated as a diocesan priest of the Archdiocese of Kingston.

I asked him whether he was frightened by the radically new direction that his life was taking after making the decisive break with the Jesuits, with whom he had spent his entire adult life to that point. His reply was instant and unstinting: "I really had no fear because I knew I had to leave the Jesuits. I didn't see any other alternative at that time. But I was very, very clear about my relationship with Christ and the word of God and I had that as my mandate. There was great, great clarity in the gospels of what must be done in our times."

The newly-formed Brothers of the Poor had a somewhat inauspicious beginning. Only six of those who had joined the retreat in the hills decided to take the initial vows on July 19, 1981. Apart from Father Ho Lung himself, the other members were Gregory Ramkissoon, who had worked closely with Father Ho Lung in the slums of Mona Common, Hayden Augustine,

a student from Trinidad, Brian Kerr, a young Jamaican, and
finally two Americans. This inauspicious beginning was soon
accentuated when both the Americans drifted off. Thus, in
the early days, the Brothers of the Poor consisted of only four
members, of whom Father Ho Lung, at the time, was the only
priest. Gregory Ramkissoon became a priest in 1984 and would
later leave the Brothers of the Poor in order to set up his own
community, "The Mustard Seed," which would cater to abandoned and disabled children; Hayden Augustine became a
priest in 1987; and Brian Kerr was ordained to the priesthood
in 1991. Father Hayden and Father Brian are, therefore, the
only members of the original band of brothers who have stayed
with Father Ho Lung from the beginning.

"Numbers actually didn't matter very much to me," says
Father Ho Lung, remembering the early days, "as long as we
were doing what was right and that Christ was pleased with our
labours. So the Lord led us step by step. No, I wasn't too worried. If I look back now and if I'd known what the Lord had in
store in the next thirty years I'd have been scared! But we just
took it step by step."

Few in number, the Brothers were also lacking in resources.
They had no money, no home, no income, and only a handful of helpers. Having taken their initial leap of faith, these
homeless mendicants found temporary accommodation in
the home of a benefactor. The four Brothers had to share one
room, into which were also packed all of Father Ho Lung's and
Gregory's books. It was cramped and entailed literally sleeping on the roof! "The books alone took up the whole room,"
laughed Father Hayden, "so we had to sleep on the roof, a flat
concrete roof. That was our house for the first two months but
we thought nothing of it, we just thought that this was the way
to go." Eventually, the Jesuit Archbishop of Kingston, Samuel

Carter, gave them the use of a former Jesuit house on Monroe Road. Later still, in 1990, a benefactor purchased for them the former Chinese school, which became known as Corpus Christi, the Brothers' first permanent base.

Much of the early work of the Brothers of the Poor revolved around ministry to the residents of the Eventide Home, which was still causing scandal more than a year after the deadly fire had destroyed one of its wards. In the summer of 1981 the annual general meeting of the Jamaican Council of Churches reported that young handicapped girls were being abducted from the wards and were being raped by their abductors. In December, Kathleen Burgess, a reporter with the *Daily Gleaner*, exposed the ongoing squalor and corruption that surrounded the home.

> Christmas is approaching and once again the spirit of good will is in the air. That was the spirit that reigned when gifts of clothes, shoes etc. were sent to the Eventide Home in November for Christmas gifts for the inmates.
>
> Unfortunately, the criminals felt no such spirit, so on 19th November they broke into the storeroom and stole everything. Of course, this was a second trip because the night before they had stolen life-saving drugs.

Having lamented the criminal activity that was adding to the misery of the Eventide residents, Burgess turned her attention to the squalid conditions in which the residents had to live:

> The place is an entire mess. It's overcrowded—two old sick people to a bed in some cases. One ward had sixty sick and old people and no toilet. . . . Many of the staff, though considerably well paid, don't care.

They were employed as a political favour, received little or no training and care even less about these sick and disabled who they are being paid to look after. The place is dirty, there are flies on some of the sick . . . it's a bad scene. . . .

I understand the idea is to move the Eventide home from the present location and there is really no alternative in the long-run but to do that, since the home is situated in a totally criminal controlled environment. The criminals . . . rape inmates and even at times steal the food out of the plates while the inmates are eating.[5]

In the midst of her gloom-laden report, Burgess mentioned that "Father Ho Lung and friends visit regularly and give cheer." In fact, giving "cheer" included wiping "messy" bottoms, binding wounds, and shaving, bathing, and feeding many of the most distressed of the residents. In this way, the band of brothers provided, week after week, solace, comfort and hope to the 700 residents living there.

In May 1982, Father Ho Lung was at the center of a heated controversy after he published—and circulated in the United States and Canada—a book of photographs showing the continuing squalor at Eventide, resulting in great embarrassment to the Jamaican government. A government minister, Alva Ross, demanded that Father Ho Lung withdraw the book from circulation because its publication was not in the Government's interest. He added that the priest had no right to send copies abroad without government permission. Ira Ashman, Kingston's deputy mayor, described the distributing of copies of the book abroad as "a deliberate plot." Father

---

5. *Daily Gleaner*, December 22, 1981.

Ho Lung responded that the "over reaction" by politicians was "childish" and that he would not withdraw the book because it was factual and because its purpose was to raise funds for the building of a new ward at the home. Furthermore, he added, the point of the book is that if people will not go to Eventide, he would take Eventide to them. The ongoing scandal needed to be exposed, including the horrific revelation that residents were literally being eaten alive by rats. In response, a high level government meeting condemned Father Ho Lung for publicizing what became known as the "Eventide rat scandal," and Ashman accused him of being part of a "conspiracy to embarrass" the local council who were responsible for running the home.[6] Although Father Ho Lung dismissed the absurdity of the conspiracy theory, he had clearly succeeded in embarrassing the government on both a local and a national level, and his exposure of its negligence added to calls for something to be done urgently about the ongoing scandal surrounding conditions at Eventide.

Outraged by his treatment at the hands of the politicians, the media rallied to Father Ho Lung's support. "Father Ho Lung . . . has a creditable track record of service on behalf of poor people," wrote a reporter in the *Daily Gleaner*. "He is a sincere man and the country could well do with more citizens like Ho Lung as well as fewer bungling bureaucracies [and] feisty politicians who have no respect for citizens' rights. . . . If what Father Ho Lung has published is true and if the press stories about rats chewing on humans are also true, how dare these petty politicians . . . challenge either the right of the press or a citizen to publish the truth."[7] Other newspapers took the

---

6. Jamaican *Daily News*, May 14, 1982.
7. *Daily Gleaner*, May 17, 1982.

same line. An editorial in the *Daily News* called for Ashman and Ross to apologize to Father Ho Lung as "the only act that would redeem their crass ingratitude and rank impertinence."[8] Another reporter asked sardonically whether the politicians would have been happier if Father Ho Lung had produced a booklet whitewashing what was happening at Eventide, publishing lies instead of the truth in order to hide the scandal from the public: "I daresay there would have been no complaint had Father Ho Lung's booklet described the conditions at Eventide in glowing terms. Maybe he should have said that the inmates were eating the rats rather than vice versa."[9]

Within a few days of this press uproar, the Prime Minister, Edward Seaga, announced plans to build the grandiose sounding Golden Age Home in a safer part of the city to which the residents of Eventide would be relocated. He also announced that Father Ho Lung would be invited to sit on the government committee overseeing the building of the new home, an appointment which was clearly a humiliating public reprimand for Alva Ross, the government minister who had originally reprimanded Father Ho Lung for publishing the book. The whole controversy had ended in a resounding moral and practical victory for Father Ho Lung and the Brothers of the Poor but also, and more importantly, it was a huge victory for the poor of Jamaica in general and for the residents of Eventide in particular.

Shortly after the controversy, a Catholic priest wrote to the *Daily Gleaner*, nominating Father Ho Lung for the annual Gleaner Honour Award, citing Father Ho Lung's "long record of dedicated service to the poor and oppressed in our society":

---

8. *Daily News*, May 18, 1982.
9. *Sunday Gleaner*, May 23, 1982.

"His booklet exposing the horrible conditions at Eventide has touched the consciences of many here and abroad and brought in a lot of money and help." The priest also mentioned the founding of the Brothers of the Poor and the blessing it had received from Archbishop Samuel Carter. He added that Father Ho Lung had "attracted many young men and women from American Colleges to come to Jamaica to help in the areas of education and social work." For these reasons, the priest concluded, "he is an inspiration of goodness to so many and good news to the poor and oppressed" and consequently deserving of the Award.[10]

A few months later, Father Ho Lung received the annual Guinness Stout Effort Award, which was presented to him at the awards ceremony at Kingston's prestigious Courtleigh Hotel on October 21. In his acceptance speech, he reminded the wealthy Jamaicans in attendance that poverty was not something of which we should be ashamed. It was a shame to neglect others but not a shame to be poor. Eventide, he stressed, was shameful because of "people's neglect of people." "As Jamaicans we have placed the people there [in Eventide]. We, the people, have forgotten our parents, our children, our brothers, our sisters. Eventide is a place for outcasts, for those we do not wish to be around. . . . We, the people of a Christian society, have not yet confronted the reality that we must serve each other and take care of our own people." The problem of Eventide, he added, was the problem of our fellowmen not caring for our own. The poor and destitute must not be forgotten.[11]

It had only been a little over a year since Father Ho Lung and a handful of like-minded souls had founded the Brothers

---

10. *Daily Gleaner* [undated, mid-1982].
11. Unidentified newspaper cutting, late October, 1982.

of the Poor. Yet, they had made a massive impact on the culture of Jamaica. Thanks to Father Ho Lung and his small band of brothers the poor and destitute would not be forgotten.

Chapter Seven

....

POLITICS AND THE POOR

DURING his acceptance speech at the Guinness Stout Effort Award dinner, Father Ho Lung discussed the other crusade on which he and the Brothers of the Poor had embarked. Apart from the tireless campaigning on behalf of the residents of Eventide Home, Father Ho Lung had begun to campaign on behalf of the young people imprisoned by Jamaica's infamous Gun Court.

The Gun Court had been established in 1974 by the Jamaican Parliament as a reactionary measure to deal with the alarming rise in gun-related crime in the early 1970s. The Court was given the power to try suspects *in camera* and without a jury. There was no provision of bail, either pre-trial or during appeal, because all defendants were considered dangerous. "Some were locked down without the possession of any firearms at all," Father Ho Lung said. "Not a bullet, not a gun, nothing. Over fifty per cent of these young men were condemned for life without any evidence of possession of firearms whatsoever."[1]

On November 15, four weeks after the Guinness Award speech, Father Ho Lung returned to the subject during a talk to the Kiwanis Club at the Jamaica Pegasus Hotel. It was a

---

1. Unidentified newspaper cutting, November 1982.

disgrace, he told the Kiwanians, that "1,500 young men who have not committed murder [will] be locked behind bars for sixteen hours a day, for the rest of their lives," unless the Gun Court Act is repealed and their cases are reviewed.

Recalling the campaign against the Gun Courts thirty years later, Father Ho Lung "sensed that this was the time to act against this gross injustice":

> I knew that a major victory had been won for the poor at Eventide. I sensed we were on a flow and the next matter was the kids who were locked up at Gun Court. A lot of people were being locked up for illegal guns, or for being in the company of people who had guns even though they themselves had none, or for living in the same yard or having friends who had guns.
>
> We kept pushing. I kept getting lots and lots of opportunities to speak in public places. Then I found out that the Minister of Justice, Winston Spaulding, had written a letter several years earlier in which he had condemned the gun court law as fundamentally unjust. I gave a number of talks reminding people that the Minister of Justice had said this and that he had now been in power for about three years and had done nothing. I called him a hypocrite.

Spaulding was furious when he read the accusations in the media. He phoned Father Ho Lung and made what the priest understood to be veiled threats.

For the second time in a number of months, Father Ho Lung's exposure of political ineptitude and hypocrisy brought quick results. Spaulding announced the government's intention to amend the Gun Court laws, paving the way for the Gun

Court Amendment Act of the following year, which led to the release of many of those who had been imprisoned. "So again, a major victory," recalled Father Ho Lung, who was at the prison teaching classes to the prisoners when the news arrived that they would finally be granted a fair trial. "All of the youngsters had just gotten letters from the government informing them that they would be having trials, and they ran up to me and we had one big celebration, laughing and partying at the prison and singing songs. It was as if the prison doors had opened, and we prayed and gave thanks."

Although this significant political victory had been won, the Brothers of the Poor continued to minister to the hundreds of young prisoners awaiting trial. From June 1981, the Brothers began weekly visits to the prisons, playing soccer with the prisoners and giving them seeds to plant. They also went from one end of the country to the other and even outside of the country to beg for help. Due to their efforts, the squalid prison, euphemistically called the Gun Court Rehabilitation Centre, was equipped with a library, established with donated funds and with books from benefactors in the United States. The prisoners themselves made the shelves.

The Brothers also started a teaching program, offering classes three days a week. Courses were offered in mathematics, English, technical drawing, and Peace and Justice. The teachers were mostly high school teachers who volunteered their services, free of charge. Father Ho Lung taught the English classes to the prisoners himself. With the help of the Master Builders Association, the Brothers of the Poor constructed a large building, divided into four classrooms with movable partitions to accommodate 180–200 student inmates. A dental program was also established and weekend prayer retreats as well as regular services were introduced. Finally the Brothers started a food program to supplement the prisoners' meager diet of yams and gravy or rice and gravy.

On November 14, 1982, in the wake of the controversies in which Father Ho Lung had become embroiled throughout the preceding months, a Sunday newspaper carried a full page feature article on his work and his beliefs. Amidst his continued and renewed call for active engagement with the needs of the poor, Father Ho Lung exhibited his loyalty to the Magisterium of the Church in his views on priestly celibacy and contraception, confirming his orthodoxy in contradistinction to the rebelliousness of many Jesuits on these issues. He told the reporter that if he had a wife and children it would inevitably restrict his activities as a priest. It was not good for a priest to be married because he would need to be a good husband and father first of all. "A married priest would have to ensure financial security for his family, and the priesthood does not reap money." A priest "should be married to the Church and have a love affair with God." Asked to comment on the thorny subject of "birth control," a bone of contention with many dissenting Catholics, Father Ho Lung echoed the teaching of the Church as defined by Pope Paul VI in his encyclical *Humanae vitae*. He told the reporter that he was all for "self-control and restraint" rather than artificial methods. "There is too much sex that does not involve love. Too many little boys and girls involved in sex that they cannot handle."[2]

Something of the spontaneity that animates Father Ho Lung's apostolate was evident on Christmas Eve 1982, when the Brothers were returning home after attending a children's Christmas party in the ghetto. It was quite late, about 11pm, and Father Ho Lung suddenly suggested that they should

---

2. Unidentified newspaper cutting, November 14, 1982.

visit the prison. Father Hayden recalls that he and the other Brothers looked at him to see if he was being serious. There was a time for visiting prisons, but surely not at 11pm on Christmas Eve. Realising that he was serious, the Brothers acquiesced and accompanied him to the prison. It says something for the respect that they had earned from the prison authorities that they were admitted at such a time and on such a night. The prisoners were of course overjoyed to receive a surprise Christmas visit and joined the Brothers in the singing of carols and the reading of scripture. Many of the prisoners literally wept for joy. "They were so moved that we came to visit them when nobody else would have, on a Christmas Eve night."

Another aspect of the life of the Brothers of the Poor was their relationship with lay volunteers, which continues to form an important part of their apostolate. One of the earliest volunteers to be attracted to Father Ho Lung and the BOP was Grace Washington. She had moved to Jamaica in January 1982 with her husband Don and had followed Father Ho Lung's work with interest in the newspapers. "Controversy whirled around him," she said, particularly with regard to Eventide and the Gun Courts:

> I kept saying to Don, "We've got to meet this man." But I didn't know how to do so. Then in January 1983, I was at Sts. Peter & Paul Catholic Church for a seminar or conference, and there was this unassuming-looking man in blue shirt and khaki pants with a wooden crucifix hanging around his neck passing out flyers: it was Fr. Ho Lung! The flyers were for two courses he was to offer to laity, one on prayer and one on psychology and religion. I look the flyer home and told Don that we were going to class.

That was the beginning. The courses were held at the brothers' house at 25 Monroe Road and went on for about three months. During that time, Father told us more about Eventide and invited us to join him and Brothers Hayden and Brian and a few others in visiting Eventide on Saturday mornings, and we did. Over time we began to join the brothers for breakfast at Monroe Road prior to going to Eventide. We were getting "hooked"!

During those early days, the Brothers hosted a once-a-month Mass for lay friends. There was a wide variety of people: a Jamaican Catholic deacon and his wife and her sister, an English couple, a Scottish couple, Don and me—all of us middle-aged or older and middle-class. There were some young Americans. There were Jamaican ex-prisoners. There were some poor Jamaicans who were from a squatter community and who worked with the Brothers. We would all gather on the verandah for Mass and then sometimes stayed on for refreshments, music, dancing.[3]

Grace Washington describes her initial attraction to Father Ho Lung and the Brothers of the Poor as being "two-pronged." On the one hand there was "a call to deeper spirituality and a serious life of prayer" and, at the same time, "a call to social justice, but not as a 'cause.'" "I had seen so many people in the United States get caught up in causes or movements and lose the spirituality that should have been informing the cause. Fr. Ho Lung seemed to have found a way to marry the two—prayer and action. That was what I was seeking."

Father Ho Lung's melding of prayer and action was

---

3. Grace Washington, correspondence with the author, January 2012.

encapsulated in the understanding of the redemptive power of suffering exhibited in an interview published in a Jamaican newspaper in February 1983. When asked why the Jesuits in Jamaica had not had a single vocation since his own entry into the Society in 1959, twenty-four years earlier, Father Ho Lung blamed the Jesuits themselves for the problem.

> The Jesuits are trying to sort themselves out. They have not yet come to grips with identifying themselves with the poor—at least not the American ones. A few years ago there was a time of great confusion in the Church, which we have not yet emerged from.
>
> In each individual there is an atmosphere of personal search. It has its positive side, but its negative side is a self-centredness, a drive for self-fulfillment which does not lay enough stress upon the right, the obligation to serve. Christianity is not meant to soothe us from suffering. Jesus went towards suffering. He himself fasted. He went to wounded humanity: the sick and the suffering. Once we call ourselves followers of Christ, we should do what He did, not avoid it. This mood [of self-centredness], I think, prevents young men from choosing the priesthood.[4]

With the wisdom of hindsight, it is easy to test the validity of Father Ho Lung's critique of the problems that beset the Church in the wake of the Second Vatican Council and see that he has been proven right. Whereas the religious congregations in the Church that embraced the "negative side," the comfort-seeking and self-centeredness, have withered in the

---

4. Unidentified newspaper cutting, February 1983.

absence of vocations, those tradition-oriented congregations that have embraced the Cross in the life of self-sacrificial service have prospered. One thinks, perhaps, of the burgeoning growth of the Nashville Dominicans, or the Dominican Sisters of Mary Mother of the Eucharist, or the Franciscan Friars of the Renewal, or the Franciscan Missionaries of the Eternal Word, each of which has reaped a rich harvest of vocations in the past thirty years. And then there are Father Ho Lung's Missionaries of the Poor, so small at the time of this interview, which would attract hundreds of vocations in the years ahead.

On February 23, a couple of weeks after the interview was published, Father Ho Lung gave a talk to the Rotary Club at the Pegasus Hotel in which he berated the government for its failure to respond to the needs of the poor. Successive governments had failed to help the nation's poor in any meaningful way, and political parties had merely used the poor as pawns to win elections. As soon as electoral victory was achieved, the poor were once again forgotten and neglected. "In every election the politicians worry about one basic people, the poor. They bury themselves with small change, with parcels of sugar and rice, and visit the people in person with smiles, hugs, and a million words and promises, which they never fulfil."[5] He criticised the People's National Party's brand of socialism, which was "quickly deteriorating into communism." The people had voted against selfish capitalism in 1974 and against non-productive socialism in 1980. Ultimately the government was not able to care for the poor, which meant that the private sector had to play a key role in bringing justice to Jamaica. The private sector in a free society has a duty to serve the poor, he said, whereas civil servants and politicians had shown that they

---

5. Unidentified newspaper cutting, February 25, 1983.

were unable or unwilling to do so. Father Ho Lung's negative appraisal of the role of politicians and government bureaucrats was caused, in part, by their obstructive attitude to the efforts of the Brothers of the Poor to assist at Eventide and in the prisons. Every hard earned success that the Brothers had achieved in the previous year on behalf of the poor had been achieved in spite of government obstruction and bureaucratic interference. "We feel everywhere we turn, the machinery of a non-productive civil service—its carcass—destroying the initiative of those who are willing and eager."[6] The problem of poverty, in Father Ho Lung's view, could not and should not be tackled by big government and the big bureaucracies that it erects. Instead, the people themselves should be empowered to help their own poorer brethren through direct action and investment unhampered by the obstructive interference of politicians and bureaucrats. Father Ho Lung soon put these principles into practice by founding independent centers run and administered directly by the Brothers of the Poor, the first of which opened the following year. In 1984, the year immortalized by George Orwell in his timely and timeless warning against the dangers of big government, Father Ho Lung would supplant Big Brother with the Brothers of the Poor.

---

6. *Daily Gleaner*, March 18, 1983.

Chapter Eight
....
THE BROKEN BODY
OF CHRIST

CONTINUING their practice of spending Christmas with the poorest of the poor, the Brothers spent the Christmas of 1983 visiting the residents of Eventide, as Grace Washington remembered:

> On Christmas Day 1983 we visited Eventide. We prepared small gifts for the residents: a roll of toilet paper, a toothbrush and toothpaste, a bar of soap. And the Brothers had mounds of donated clothes. Don and I joined the Brothers, and we were all honoured by the presence of Archbishop Carter. We visited each ward of Eventide giving out the little gifts to each person. I remember observing Fr. Ho Lung grabbing garments from huge plastic bags and thrusting them at random into the hands of waiting people as he passed by. Later, Father told me how pleased the Archbishop had been.[1]

In January 1984, Father Ho Lung spent three weeks at the University of Scranton in Pennsylvania teaching a course on

---

1. Grace Washington, correspondence with the author.

the Christian Mission of the Third World, as part of his own ongoing mission to raise the awareness of Americans and Canadians to the plight of the world's poor.

Returning to Jamaica, he resumed the day-to-day work with the island's poor, visiting Eventide and overseeing the building of the BOP's first center for the destitute and handicapped, scheduled to be opened later the same year. His own passion for the poor was evident in the description of an encounter with a dying man in Eventide:

> Joe Charlton was covered with sores . . . His skin was jet black, but pink sores were all over him. His entire face, hands, legs—yes, even his belly and back—were covered with yellow pus and scabs. It was a miracle that out of his near corpse could come breath and a voice, "You pray for me, Father."
>
> "Yes, Joe."
>
> "And how is the day?" He couldn't tell because he was blind.
>
> "It is beautiful."
>
> "What bring for me today?" he asked cheerfully.
>
> "I have some milk and a half-bar of soap and toothpaste."
>
> "That is useful and very kind of you."
>
> I looked at the pathetic figure: the arms and legs paralyzed—stiff dried sticks—and the tall gaunt figure and the face with eyes gone blind and lips puffy. He was only fit for burial, and the maggots the Brothers cleaned had gotten a head start. . . .
>
> I took Joe's hand but with feelings of revulsion. His fingers curled and held onto my fingers. The warmth and love from his body flowed from his fingers into mine. I closed my other hand over his and didn't worry about the pus. And love warmed

me through and through. This is the infusion of the Holy Spirit, and God's grace filling me with divine life.[2]

For Father Ho Lung "the image of that man covered with sores and dying coalesced with the image of Christ on the Cross. . . . Silently, I thanked him for bringing Christ to me . . . We had shared as brothers the broken body of Christ in Mr. Charlton." These few words reveal the secret of Father Ho Lung's love for the poor and the key to understanding the passion and sweat that drives the apostolate of the Missionaries of the Poor. If the Crucified Christ is visible in the broken bodies and broken hearts of the poor and disabled, then it should be a joy for Christians to lay down their lives for their poor and broken brothers and sisters. This is the reason that Father Ho Lung denies stridently that he and the Brothers are social workers. They are not merely workers in the vineyard but servants of the broken body of Christ. Their work with the poor is not merely a job or a duty but a labor of love. They are laying down their lives for their friends.

One of Father Ho Lung's many charismatic gifts is his ability to convey to the Brothers and to the lay helpers of the MOP the beauty of God's love in the midst of the ugliness of suffering. This ability had a great impact on Grace Washington:

> I was especially drawn to Father's insistence that we need to look at evil and the dark side of life and see it for what it is. (You have to look into the eyes of a murderer and know that he is a murderer and then love him, for he, too, is a child of God.) Going to Eventide with the brothers and then working at

---

2. Fr. Richard Ho Lung, *Diary of a Ghetto Priest*, Kingston, Jamaica: Missionaries of the Poor, 1998, pp. 11–12.

Faith Centre and the subsequent centres, I was constantly meeting the dark side. Faith Centre became for me light in the darkness, Bethlehem upon which shone the star in the dark night. And even at Faith Centre there was the wonder of such things as knowing that that old man sitting in the shade had been an abortionist and yet we loved him and cared for his needs.[3]

Once one understands the passion with which Father Ho Lung loves the poor, it is easy to understand his frustration and anger at the indifference of politicians, bureaucrats, and the rich. Father Ho Lung's frustration was palpable in an encounter with an old school friend, a Catholic, who had become very rich but was blind to the needs of the poor and to his responsibility to help meet those needs. The old friend had asked him to come and bless his house. Father Ho Lung agreed and asked in turn if the wealthy friend could pay for a couple of bags of cornmeal to feed the poor. To his surprise, the friend hesitated, complaining that "things were tight" but that he would manage to find the necessary funds. Here's how Father Ho Lung recounted the story in his "Diary":

> I was picked up in a Rolls Royce. I understand that a Rolls Royce, if importation is allowed, costs 1.5 million Jamaican dollars; that is nearly 40,000 US dollars. An entire family of five in the ghetto with the mother fully employed have to live on $125 a week or about four U.S. dollars. Two bags of cornmeal, five people's lives over and against the cost of a vehicle!

---

3. Grace Washington, correspondence with the author.

Is this our island's value system? Certainly it is to this Christian gentleman. . . .

When I went to the goodly gentleman's house, a favour I did because he had been a school-mate of mine and a Catholic, I was shocked. The house was built on the side of a hill: three stories high, twenty-four rooms. It reminded me of a Chinese pagoda. Red ceiling tiles contrasted with the pure white of the rest of the house. The entire building, my host stated, was imported from the Far East: fine bone china, ivory, burnished gold, and brass. The tables and chairs were moulded by hand, lacquered and carved in gold and black. Delicate carvings and vases, silk flowers, artificial but beautifully shaped, were placed in the drawing and dining rooms, screened with silken drapes. The yard simulated an oriental garden: plants shaped along horizontal lines, goldfish ponds, rocks, peacocks. A Chinese emperor's home.

There was hesitation when I had asked for two bags of cornmeal for the poor.[4]

Indignation pulsated through every line of the ghetto priest's description of his close encounter with opulence. There seems to be a grating incongruity between the personality of the gen-tle-voiced priest and the anger seething beneath the surface of these words. It is, however, a justifiable and righteous anger akin to the anger that Christ showed as he drove the money-changers from the temple. It is not the anger, born of envy, of Marxist class warriors. It is clear from his essay that Father Ho Lung's anger was not driven by jealousy. He began by praising Air Jamaica and American Airlines for allowing those involved

---

4. Ho Lung, *Diary of a Ghetto Priest*, pp. 144–45.

with the Brothers of the Poor to travel free of charge to the United States:

> Air Jamaica said, "Yes." They want to help us with our projects for the poor. American Airlines is also a tremendous help. Our overseas concerts are a splendid source of revenue, not to mention the wonderful fellowship among the singers, musicians, audiences, and organizers. Nobody gets any pay, nobody wants any pay: all goes to the poor and to no one else. Air Jamaica had no hesitation: all three overseas journeys would be paid for. They know that our poor are in need. Air Jamaica even sent a nurse, once weekly, to minister to our sick. Food, clothes, and an assortment of goods abandoned at the airport come our way.
>
> We have other generous benefactors who are prominent in the business community. I do not condemn businessmen or their opinions. I do condemn selfishness, however, and I do encounter selfishness among the rich. I meet selfishness in the poor as well, but the selfish poor are not in a position to help.[5]

Clearly, Father Ho Lung doesn't condemn wealth, but selfishness. And he reminds the wealthy of the words of the Gospel that more is expected from those to whom more has been given.[6]

As the allusion to the overseas concerts attests, Father Ho Lung had resumed the musical dimension of his ministry. From 1976 until 1984, with the exception of the Christmas production in 1980, the reggae priest had made way for the ghetto

---

5. Ibid., p. 143.
6. Luke 12:48.

priest. Feeling that the music was a distraction from his primary vocation to the poor, Father Ho Lung had sought to lay his Muse aside and concentrate on his work. He found, however, that his Muse would not be ignored, but insisted on being heard. Melodies kept coming to his mind and would not be silenced. Eventually he realized that the music was a God-given gift that should be used to help with his ministry. Through the music the message could be spread far and wide and money could be raised for the poor. Thus, every year from 1984 to the present, Father Ho Lung has written and produced new musical reviews, bringing the music of praise and the ministry to the poor into synchronized harmony.

On July 23, 1984, Father Ho Lung spoke again at the Rotary Club. Like his speech a year earlier, his subject was the plight of the nation's poor and the responsibility of the business community to help. On this occasion, however, his explication of the subsidiarist solution to the problem was even clearer:

> I ask you: our talented businessmen, that though you are experiencing difficulties yourselves, to organize programmes, sponsored by you and your business, to create small productive programmes for our poor. . . . Let me state that small projects are what we really need and is best for our country. . . . The government does not, cannot and will not provide for our street people and the poor. That leads to one option—you must provide. You must seize this country, make it your own, you must claim the poor people as your own. The government wins elections by pretending it can take care of the poor of our island. You, the private people, must realize that when you claim this country and claim the

> people, then and only then will our country be free
> and safe.
>
> As long as politics runs everything and pre-
> tends to run everything, we are in danger, great
> danger. . . . We are a country polarized and com-
> pletely controlled by politics. It is vital the country
> be decentralized and depoliticized, by you, the pri-
> vate people, taking control of our people. It is our
> country at stake. You must seize the power, and you
> must take over, and this Jamaica will be a country
> run by the people rather than by the politicians.[7]

A few weeks after this strident speech calling for private citizens to bypass the politicians in promoting and financing self-
help programmes for the poor, one of the fruits of this dynamic,
subsidiarist approach was the opening of the first center by the
Brothers of the Poor.

In September 1984, Father Ho Lung opened Faith Centre, a
chapel and community residence for the destitute in the heart
of the ghetto. Blessed by the Catholic Archbishop of Kingston,
Samuel Carter, upon its opening, it would be the first of the
many missionary outreaches for which the Missionaries of the
Poor are known. Father Ho Lung's vision for Faith Centre was
of Bethlehem in the slums. Into the darkness of the poverty
and violence of the slums, a light would shine as on Bethlehem.
At Faith Centre, twelve destitute people from the surrounding
slums would receive a new home, and there would follow the
first twenty people to leave Eventide. There would be a free sec-
ondary school for poor boys who otherwise would not be able
to go on to high school and also work projects for people in the
community with no jobs. There would be soup for poor people,

---

7. Unidentified press cutting, July 27, 1984.

and food lines, and a community center and a place of worship. It would be a microcosm of the world of the poor.

Father Ho Lung and the small band of lay volunteers had visited Eventide to survey potential residents. In keeping with Father Ho Lung's kaleidoscopic world-view, the people selected represented young adults with varying forms of physical and mental disabilities—cerebral palsy, Down syndrome, autism. There were adults with schizophrenia, and blind, crippled, and mute young adults, as well as a few elderly people. The people selected from the neighborhood were all elderly.[8]

Part of Father Ho Lung's vision for Faith Centre was to build bridges between the first world and the third world and between lay people and religious. Thus it was that there were from the beginning lay volunteers: American, Canadian, British, and Jamaican. Early volunteers included a retired Mennonite couple, the husband being put in charge of building the log cabin chapel and the wife volunteering as a teacher; a young Italian American who did just about anything that needed to be done; another Mennonite who was in charge of the weaving project and later became the manager of the preliminary construction at Jacob's Well, the next BOP center to be opened; a Canadian couple who volunteered to nurse and teach; and another Canadian who built the school.

The depths of passion and anger that Father Ho Lung felt at this time is evident in the address he gave at the official opening of Faith Centre:

> Each community in this island, if it be truly Christian, needs to give up some of its space, some of its land, some of its goods, to the poor. . . . Is it not

---

8. I am indebted to Grace Washington for these memories of the founding of Faith Centre.

a displeasure to God Himself that so many worship Him and so few serve their neighbour?

Is it that Christianity is dead in the hearts of the churches in Jamaica? In our island in which there is such dire poverty, I challenge every church to have a home for the destitute, no matter how small. In relation to the church's size and its wealth, there can and must be a home for the destitute, for the outcast, for the dying, for the blind, for the homeless.

Christianity cannot be a matter of the worshipping community praying together and giving God thanks for His blessings and His mercy. If it becomes that, it is not a community that follows Christ. . . . Christianity in that context is without love of neighbour. But what about the Crucified Christ— Riverton City, Trench Town, Mona Common? The thousands of homeless, the squatters, the jobless?

Until we take care of the poor, God will not bless our Church, and should not bless our Church. We would be empty sounds and tinkling cymbals. Until we take care of our old, the dying, the homeless, the destitute, we shall not be Christian. . . .

Christ Himself commanded, "Love one another as I have loved you"; "Greater love no man has, than to lay down his life for his friends."

The Christian faith . . . becomes true when it addresses itself, not by word, but by deeds. Priests and parsons, sisters and deacons, all religious leaders who preach the word and do nothing, are leaders who resemble the hypocrites of Christ's times. . . . In many ways we betray Christ and the Church, for our word is not made flesh. We tell the people in words what to do without doing it ourselves.[9]

As with his earlier indignation at the selfishness of the rich Catholic businessman, Father Ho Lung's broadside against the "scribes, Pharisees and hypocrites"[10] of lukewarm Christianity gives the impression of harshness that is not really representative of the true gentleness and meekness of his character. The latter was much more in evidence in a talk given at a Christmas dinner in December 1984 in which he said that "only service and selflessness can transform our world" and that "there is no other meaning to life but to serve God and our fellowmen." Furthermore, he declared that "there is no happier life than to serve our brothers and sisters, and to feed, wash and clothe those who are desolate as to do this is to feed, clothe and wash the Body of Christ." Getting to the heart of the Christmas spirit, he stated that Christ's coming to Bethlehem changed everything. "The life of Jesus Christ has decreed that service through self sacrifice is the only meaning to life." He ended by accentuating the paradox that true happiness can only be found through suffering: "One cannot find happiness unless he or she serves, sacrifices or lives on behalf of others or until we give until there's nothing left."[11] As another Christmas arrived, reminding the ghetto priest of the birth of the love that changed everything, he must surely have been one of the happiest men on earth.

---

9. Unidentified newspaper cutting, June 20, 1980.
10. Matthew 23:13 ff.
11. Unidentified newspaper cutting, December 19, 1984.

Chapter Nine

....

AN INSPIRATIONAL MOTHER

"I DON'T know why, but I've found describing Father challenging. Perhaps this is because to be in his presence is to be in the presence of mystery. One senses deep, abiding faith in him and deep peace. Here is someone who is intimate with the Lord and yet meets you as a faithful friend and a warm and funny human being."[1] Grace Washington's description of Father Ho Lung illuminates the other side of his character, all too easily overlooked in the midst of his busy and controversial public life. And yet, it is this man of faith and peace who is known and loved by those who have joined him in his work with the poor, whether as fully fledged Brothers or as lay helpers.

Grace Washington—one of the most active lay helpers during the early years—attended numerous three-day retreats in the 1980s that Father Ho Lung gave in Jamaica to small groups of lay people. The retreatants included supporters from Canada, England, and the United States, as well as lay volunteers in Jamaica, and workers and weavers from the Faith Centre. She was surprised to recall how often Father Ho Lung gave these retreats and further, how often he gave her individual spiritual direction and retreats. "Even as he was establishing the

---

1. Grace Washington, correspondence with the author.

Brothers of the Poor and searching high and low for vocations, Father gave of himself so generously to these lay people." Once Faith Centre was begun, there were even retreats for the workers and weavers. "And he called out of us so much, challenging us to be serious about building the kingdom of God, especially among the poor. Yet even as he challenged us to embrace the cross and self-sacrifice and not to be mediocre Christians, we celebrated! We had fun! We laughed! He has a great sense of humour. He can be and is very serious, but he can also be playful. He is dedicated and has a deep sense of faithfulness and commitment." Many of these retreats were held at the Jamaica Defence Force camp up in the mountains at Newcastle, the same place at which the initial retreat was held in 1981, which gave birth to the Brothers of the Poor. "The facilities were a bit primitive, but it was beautiful, and we were all deeply moved."

> For me personally, I am so grateful for the way that Father brought (and brings) together Christ's love of the poor, facing squarely the reality of darkness and evil, and a faith that has intellectual integrity. As I reviewed my notes, I was struck by the references Father made to such figures as Kierkegaard, Dostoevsky, Jung, Merton, Hopkins, and his beloved T.S. Eliot. But he did so not as an intellectual or academic exercise. No, he gave them flesh, made them live, so as to enliven a passage of scripture or a point for meditation.

Throughout 1985 and 1986, Father Ho Lung continued to beseech the politicians, especially the two party leaders, Michael Manley and Edward Seaga, to bury their differences for the good of the nation. He also continued to call on Jamaica's business leaders to offer practical help for the poor. Whereas

Manley and Seaga paid little heed, seeking to bury the hatchet in each other's head, the business community responded positively. Throughout this period the Faith Centre received many valuable donations from Jamaica's businesses.

In June 1986 a newspaper columnist wrote that Father Ho Lung's work had still not been officially honored by the Jamaican government. Whilst he had received awards from business entities, such as Guinness, he had never been honored by the nation.

> How many of us would take it upon ourselves to go into some of the stinking, neglected homes run by the government, ignoring the foul smell . . . while we clean up the dirty old people who live there? I remember going to the Eventide Home one day and the stench that reached me from the gate was suffocating. But inside one of the nastiest, most unhygienic and depressing wards I have ever seen, was Father Richard Ho Lung. . . . He was cutting their toenails which had grown almost two inches long and were full of dirt. After cleaning up the people he and his colleagues fed them and played the guitar for them. He did this often - without the fuss or fanfare so many persons require when they are doing the slightest of deed. I stumbled on the whole thing.

The reporter wrote of the attacks that Father Ho Lung had endured from politicians when he had published the book of photographs of the appalling conditions at Eventide in order to raise money to improve the conditions of those living there; something that the politicians who were responsible for Eventide had failed to do. "He did raise money. In fact the people at the pleasant Golden Age Home which replaced Eventide, are there largely because of the efforts of Father Ho Lung."

In addition to Golden Age Home, the reporter also described Faith Centre, established by the Brothers of the Poor two years earlier as "a palace for those poor and indigent who are housed there. Many people eat because of the soup kitchen he operates there daily. People who were sleeping on the dirt floor in cardboard houses now have sturdy wooden houses that he has helped them to erect." She praised the priest's crucial role in amending the Gun Court law, which led to the release of many people from prison, and praised his role in helping to rehabilitate those who were thus released. "I could go on and on to talk about the achievements of this humble man Father Ho Lung."[2]

During the summer of 1986 construction began on a hospice at Faith Centre. Although it was built with cancer patients in mind, it become increasingly a place where those dying of AIDS could end their days with dignity, surrounded by love and prayer. The building, erected with blocks made by the Brothers of the Poor, contains a four room school building as well as a place reserved for the terminally ill. At the same time that the hospice was being built, work was being done on a new center—called Jacob's Well—for the destitute and homeless in nearby Hanover Street, which would accommodate forty residents. Father Ho Lung explained that they had "raised enough money from our concerts to buy the building there."[3]

A journalist who visited Faith Centre in July 1986 was deeply affected by the experience in a way that those who have been there will instantly recognize:

> Much has already been written of Father Ho Lung's indefatigable efforts and how beloved he is to the poor and those who feel there is little hope in living.

---

2. Unidentified newspaper cutting, June 30, 1986.
3. *Sunday Gleaner Magazine*, August 3, 1986.

> To actually witness the way children and adults cling to him and follow him about is to witness what it really means to talk about a shepherd and his sheep. Simply to be in his company means that you are a target for displays of affection also. If you visit them, don't be unnerved if little Charles, who is a deaf mute, comes laughing up to you to run his hands through your hair, or if one of the several young girls, who are severely retarded, slips a shy hand in yours to whisper hello.[4]

Father Ho Lung explained to the reporter that Faith Centre was not a mere charitable institution where people could expect a free handout. It was not an impersonal institution but a living, breathing human community in which each member contributed, according to his or her abilities. "I tell them," explained Father Ho Lung, "if you don't work, you don't eat." Even the beds on which the residents slept were built by the community, and a weaving workshop using scraps donated by textile companies was producing mats for sale. The journalist was particularly taken with one female resident, nineteen-year-old Arthurine, who was paralyzed in the arms but used her toes to weave the mats.

Apart from their work for the destitute, homeless and handicapped in the centers, the Brothers also reached out to the poor of the ghetto by helping them to repair their homes, either by laying down concrete floors of by using timber donated to the centers to patch walls and roofs. "We don't actually build complete houses," said Father Ho Lung, "except in the one or two cases when the people are on the street and have no shelter at all."

---

4. Ibid.

The journalist's feature article on the work of the Brothers of the Poor prompted a glowing leading article in the *Sunday Gleaner* on August 3, praising the work of the Brothers and concluding thus: "The Brothers and the benefactors who support them seek to build in the ghettoes of despair monuments of faith and caring that should inspire imitation elsewhere. Their example is practical self-reliance, so often preached but seldom practiced where it matters most: amongst the poorest in our society." Once again, Father Ho Lung's adherence to Catholic social teaching, especially with respect to subsidiarity, was reaping practical benefits for the poor whilst also winning the respect and admiration of the wealthy. It was also earning the respect of the poorest of the poor, as another journalist discovered whilst walking with Father Ho Lung through the toughest, poorest and most violent parts of the Kingston ghetto.

> As we tour the ghettoes, youth idling on the streets shout enthusiastically, "Father Ho Lung," "Father." Some of the toughest, crudest-looking people speak to him with reverence and absolute politeness. . . . Meeting Richard Ho Lung is like meeting a whirlwind: one does not emerge unruffled. We can't be in his presence without being gripped with a passion for the poor, without a sense of transcendence. He speaks in a quiet, melodic voice but his words loudly rattle the nerves of the unjust and uncaring.
>
> "Long life Father! Long live Father!" An inmate from the Gun Court shouts from the playfield. Another inmate, on another occasion, says the exact words, adding "inside here and outside you are just a great man."
>
> In the ghetto, he calls to some identified bad men in the area who respond to him immediately. "I am

fighting hard against the ganja and cocaine here. The drugs are a big problem here," he says. The area along Gold Street, Hanover Street and Laws Street is particularly violent, he says. Does he fear his life, especially as he is now fighting a drug ring? "Oh no!" he brushes off the question. "I have to die for something."[5]

*   *   *

Considering his mission to offer free service to the poorest of the poor, it is not surprising that Father Ho Lung is often associated with Mother Teresa. Indeed he is sometimes called the "male Mother Teresa." In 1985, Mother Teresa's Missionaries of Charity opened a center in the Kingston ghetto, only a few blocks away from the centers run by the Brothers of the Poor. In 1986, when Mother Teresa visited Jamaica to officially launch the new center, one of the Missionary sisters called Father Ho Lung, telling him that Mother Teresa would like to visit Faith Centre. "We had a little broken down van so we picked her up," Father Ho Lung said.

> She was at exposition of the Blessed Sacrament when we arrived. It was in the afternoon. I think maybe about three or four o'clock in the afternoon. She came to meet us, and while we were driving up to Faith Centre some gunmen came around and, poor soul, they frightened her a little bit, but she was peaceful. She was quite peaceful, and really they respected her. They just swarmed the car. As she came into Faith Centre she was almost like a child, the way she embraced the residents. There were

5. *Sunday Gleaner*, May 31, 1987.

many who had Down syndrome, many cripples and some elderly people and so forth. She just walked around and played with them, and then she sat down, and then she began to talk to them and talk to the brothers about prayer and about her own life.

She stayed for about an hour.

"She was marvelous," Father Ho Lung said, remembering the encounter twenty-five years later. "She just had that sparkle in her eyes that could only come from something very deep within, very bright although an old lady. She was so full of life and a sense of joy. That was a very, very, very significant meeting. We walked together, and it was just nice being with her. Then we brought her back, but of course that was one of the two greatest moments of my life, I think, in terms of meeting with people." The other great moment was meeting Pope John Paul II a few years later.

Father Hayden recalls that Father Ho Lung had always been "very inspired" by Mother Teresa and her apostolate and wanted to see more of her while she was in Jamaica. He requested that he and some of the Brothers be allowed to visit her in the new center. "She invited us to come," says Father Hayden. "We spent an hour sitting on the floor Indian-style, which shocked me because we hadn't gone to India yet." The meeting consisted mainly of Father Ho Lung asking questions and Mother Teresa giving responses. All the while, Father Ho Lung was taking notes, hoping to learn as much as he could from the holy woman's experiences.

"She encouraged us to be the male counterpart of her order," said Father Ho Lung, "which I thought about for awhile, but we were different. Her primary thrust, I think, is with the elderly and the dying. She does take care of children, though, as I

AN INSPIRATIONAL MOTHER 107

found out later. But that was her first primary thrust. We like to build communities. We like to link people together, because we figure that loneliness is the greatest suffering of the homeless people. So from the inception we wanted to have people relate to each other of different ages, and also we wanted our brothers relating to the people in that way. We want them to be true brothers to these people not to be so much workers. We also wanted our homes to be a place of prayer so that even the homeless themselves must pray. We want people to be singing and that there be informal services and even some formal services within the homes every day."

The two principal differences, therefore, between Father Ho Lung's Missionaries, and Mother Teresa's Missionaries lay in community and evangelization. Father Ho Lung's vision was for the residents at the centers to form a community, a family, of which the Brothers were themselves a seamless part. Communities needed the interaction of young and old, the physically fit and the physically disabled, in such a way that each learned to love and help his neighbor. Furthermore, whereas Mother Teresa's Missionaries of Charity shied away from open evangelization of the poor whom they served, largely due to their ministry in non-Christian countries where such evangelization might be seen as insensitive or even provocative, the Missionaries of the Poor were unabashed in the evangelical dimension of their apostolate. I witnessed, for instance, the shameless way Father Ho Lung reminded a pregnant woman visiting Holy Innocents, a center for pregnant mothers opened by the Missionaries of the Poor in 2011, that she should go to church. On discovering that the lady in question was a Protestant of some shape or shade, he urged her to start going to the Catholic Church, reminding her that it was the Catholics who had provided the free ultrasound services that she was using. I felt almost bashful, and was almost blushing, at the sheer chutzpah of his Catholic evangelism. It was, however, refreshing to see such unapologetic zeal in the desire to win converts to the Faith. Having seen this encounter between the enthusiastic missionary and the non-believer, I could see why the quiet understatement of Mother Teresa's charism would not suit the exuberance of Father Ho Lung's desire to win souls for Christ.

Father Hayden recalls fondly Mother Teresa's visit but remembers that, even in those days, Father Ho Lung had stated emphatically that he was not a male Mother Teresa. His insistence was partly in deference to Mother Teresa herself, recognizing that he was not worthy to be her counterpart. *Domine, non sum dignus.* And yet, says Father Hayden, "I think he also wanted to insist on our distinctiveness *vis-à-vis* the Missionaries of Charity, that we were not necessarily a male counterpart of the MC Sisters because we do have something that is distinctive even from them." Asked to elaborate, he echoed the view of Father Ho Lung regarding the dimension of evangelism: "Our outreach is different. They don't do that kind of outreach. They don't do evangelization the way we do. They're not as, I wouldn't want to use the word aggressive, but . . ." He paused for a moment, thinking of the best way to explain. He then spoke of the MOP Mission in Uganda, telling me that they counted 110 Muslims at one of their ceremonies. They are not abashed evangelizing their non-Christian brothers and sisters.

Father Hayden also echoed Father Ho Lung by highlighting the differences in the way the Missionaries of the Poor and the Missionaries of Charity run their respective centers. Father Ho Lung "wanted that atmosphere which the MC Sisters would not have. They are much more institutional, whereas we have young and old, male and female, you know, there's much more animation. I don't want to criticize them but to consider the difference in the way they run their centers and the way we run ours. There's a little more engagement, much more interaction in the way that we do things. We talk about building community." The Missionaries of Charity were more somber and quiet. "It probably fits into the Indian rituals, culturally. Quiet and peace." Father Hayden stressed that it's not a question of which charism is better than the other, but simply a question of recognizing real differences in the respective apostolates.

No, Father Ho Lung is not a male Mother Teresa. He was, however, for a few short hours in 1986 her disciple, learning the lessons that she could teach. Father Ho Lung might not be a male Mother Teresa, but Mother Teresa is still an inspirational mother to the Brothers of the Poor.

Chapter Ten

THE LIVES AND LOVES
OF THE GHETTO

O N July 5, 1987, Father Ho Lung returned to St. George's
College, his alma mater and the school at which he had
taught for many years, to give the commencement address.
Although the call of the poor had led him away from the academic life, his passion for education remained undiminished.
In an article for the *Daily Gleaner*, Ho Lung lamented the
replacement of the classic liberal arts by the heartless dictates
of utilitarianism:

> What is education today? . . . And what of the
> schooling of the heart? The humanities which
> arouse and inform our sense of pity and love have
> been abrogated to that one intention: to build up
> personal security. . . . Today the humanizing which
> the arts are meant to accomplish is labeled useless.
>
> No matter how rich, no matter how brilliant we
> are . . . once the heart stops beating, a man is dead.
> Love is what stirs the heart and keeps a man alive . . .
>
> I believe our humanity is finally tested by our
> ability to love, by the greatness of our hearts. The
> more we can love, the more people we can serve

with joy—especially the grotesque and the out-cast—the more human we become.[1]

Love is what stirs the heart and keeps a man alive. . . . If this maxim is true, and it is, then Father Ho Lung is truly "a man alive." His ability to love, especially the grotesque and the out-cast, was made known in a regular feature column in the *Daily Gleaner*, "Diary of a Ghetto Priest," which he began to write in 1987. When confronted with Father Ho Lung's eloquence and with the gutsy passion with which he pours himself out in love for the poor, I feel that there is nothing his biographer can do but to point to him and be silent. This, therefore, is what I propose to do, allowing Father Ho Lung's "Diary" to speak for itself. Here is Father Ho Lung's vivid description of the arrival of Joel, an autistic child, to Faith Centre:

> The policeman had cradled in his lap a little boy child. . . . The policeman was muscular but like a mother: it was an image of the biblical lion carrying in his arms the lamb.
>
> "We don't know his name, Father. What will you call him?"
>
> "Joel. The prophet."
>
> The policeman laughed a hearty approval. He handed the boy over to our nurse Anne Maria as gentle as could be.
>
> "The mother, we believe, is from Sligoville. We can't find her. Joel is a twin child. The mother left off this child but has with her the other one. We might also have to bring the other to you."
>
> Little Joel. What a sad little face! Both eyes are turned upwards towards the top of his head. He has

---

1. Ho Lung, *Diary of a Ghetto Priest*, pp. 147–48.

a "bang" belly: swollen with a big navel and stick-like arms and legs. Our nurse told me he is malnourished and full of worms. He is severely autistic and speaks not a word. He beats his head against the solid wall or against the floor. He seems partially paralyzed on the entire left side of his body, and drags his left leg when he walks. Always he has his left arm crooked as if it were hanging in a sling, and it is stiff with his fingers closed like a claw.

If I had to guess, Joel is four years old. He is not toilet trained, so he has to be led or lifted to the toilet. In his stool, I saw blood, due to internal bleeding we were to find out later. The blood was congealed in dark blotches. The policeman had said that the mother was known to beat Joel terribly.

Marvin, our little Down's [sic] syndrome boy, and Peter, a physically disabled but bright little boy, came up to Joel. They were quiet and gentle in their approach, but Joe shied away in a panic and hit at them. Joel never seems to smile and never looks anyone in the face. In fact, he likes to be left alone and often he returns to a corner in the dormitory or in the office and just continuously bashes his head against the desk or the wall. At other times, he finds himself a place in the glazing sun and lies down, curled up like a little butterfly, and sleeps. Beads of sweat pour out of him, but Joel does not move.

Peter and Marvin are fully alive with their lust for living although Peter is crippled and Marvin is not very intelligent. But they seem to know what is happening to Joel: that he needs his space, that they mustn't be too rough or too friendly, that Joel needs time to trust them and become part of the family.

Anne Maria has found a way of playing with him. She tickles him with a light touch. He laughs. She tickles him a little more. He giggles and gurgles. She tickles him a whole heap, and he laughs heartily. In Anne Maria, Joe has found a mother. Now he climbs into her lap and plays with her fingers and hugs her warmly. He is like a little butterfly slowly unfolding in the warmth of her motherly love.

Motherhood. In a time when modern women are becoming like men—office-bound, businesslike, efficient, and even hard—the children of our world will lose out. They will lose compassion, tenderness, and the intuitive powers of loving without reserve, without reason, without condition.[2]

Father Ho Lung's lament for the destruction of motherhood is also a lament for the child abuse that is its inevitable consequence. In a society that has deified a woman's right to choose selfishly, it is the children who suffer. Whereas Joel was beaten mercilessly by a mother who felt handicapped by her son's disability, Frankie, a young man with Down syndrome, had been brutalized and deserted by his mother for being born with "the brain of a fool." Frankie's aunt, Alice, left him at Faith Centere and told Father Ho Lung that Frankie's mother had emigrated to England. When Frankie was a baby, Alice said, his mother used to "hide the boy child in her back room and lock him up":

Frankie used to sit down as if in a prison. And when people wasn't around, him used to sweep the house and the backyard. But Violet used to take set on him; she hated him like sin. Poor Frankie couldn't do any harm. Him would just smile and say, 'Mama, don't hit me' . . .

2.   Ho Lung, *Dairy of a Ghetto Priest*, pp. 20–22.

Alice left Frankie with us. He is a big baby whale who flops around and gives everybody a hug. He and the other Down's syndrome men are our welcoming committee at Faith Centre. Everybody who comes to visit us will be greeted by a great big smile, a handshake, and a hug, all dealt out with absolute trust and a confidence that love is the most obvious of activities.

Father Ho Lung recalled one of the regular visits that Frankie received from his brother, a tall slender Rastafarian, whose hair was "all dreadlocks, long and wrapped in torches, in celebration of his defiance against society": "They spent the day together. The rastaman really loves his brother Frankie. They had arms around each other all day long. When the day was done, he held Frankie's hand and wished him good-bye. Frankie enveloped his brother with a hug and mushy kiss. All the defiance of the rastaman melted away." Frankie was so overjoyed that his brother had come that he went around telling everybody:

Frankie and the Down's syndrome residents are by definition, love. But they are not . . . stupid. They have an instinctive sense of right and wrong. They also possess a deep sense of fairness and justice. These beautiful Down's syndrome people are very special children: God's children. They live on love, and they live to love. They are basic elemental human nature, in all its beauty and simplicity. We know that if anyone has a Down's syndrome child, they can be sure that joy, laughter, and love have been given to them as a special gift from God. We welcome these gifts with delight.[3]

---

3. Ibid., pp. 49–52.

As the father of Leo, a child with Down syndrome, I can heartily endorse Father Ho Lung's words. Leo is indeed a special gift from God and he has been the bringer of joy, laughter, and love to our family, as well as the setter of many challenges, the latter of which, though painful on occasion, have benefited us more than all the laughter and joy. Someone told me recently that most of us are given life in order to learn but that some very special people are given life in order to teach. Children with Down syndrome are, in accordance with this profoundly true definition, very special people. They are here to teach the rest of us about love, not merely in the "feel-good" sense in which the word is so often abused in our largely loveless world, but in the self-sacrificial sense, which is the heart of love's deepest meaning. If the true definition of love is to lay down one's life for the other, the child with Down syndrome or with other challenging disabilities teaches us how to love more fully and more truly. Can there be a greater gift to any family than the gift of this very special love? This being so, how wicked is the world in which we now live, a world which systematically exterminates children with Down syndrome and other disabilities? How wicked is a world which enshrines the "right" of a mother to choose to kill her own unborn children? How wicked is a world which systematically discriminates against the weak, the infirm and the disabled by encouraging mothers to kill their own "imperfect" babies? Once again, Father Ho Lung encapsulates the heart and hub of the problem:

> There are so many worries in the world because our modern world requires that we have so much. We sophisticated people battle and compete to acquire so much, intellectually and financially. . . . There are so many goods that are there to be had; so we miss

the flowers, the trees, the birds of the air, and each other.

There is no ambition, no battle for power, no pomp, no falsehood, no hypocrisy in the Down's syndrome people.[4]

Referring to Garth, another man with Down syndrome at Faith Centre, Father Ho Lung connects the beautiful simplicity of those with Down syndrome with the beautiful and simple things in life: "I like going to the beach with Garth. I find in him the way to regain innocence. With him, I can delight in Brother Sun, Sister Moon, the pelicans and the clouds sailing in the clear blue sky. And I can float on the ocean of faith, buoyed up by God's grace and His fatherly love."[5] For Father Ho Lung, as for all people who see those with Down syndrome with the eyes of love, Frankie and Garth were not only blessings to those fortunate enough to know them, but were teachers of a priceless truth about God and His Creation.

---

4. Ibid., p. 53.
5. Ibid. p. 54.

Chapter Eleven

....

HUMAN TRAGEDY AND
DIVINE COMEDY

For I saw that finny goblin
Hidden in the abyss untrod;
And I knew there can be laughter
On the secret face of God.
Blow the trumpets, crown the sages,
Bring the age by reason fed!
(He that sitteth in the heavens,
"He shall laugh"—the prophet said.)
　　　　　　—G. K. Chesterton (From "The Fish")

ON SEPTEMBER 12, 1988, Hurricane Gilbert slammed into Jamaica, no doubt reminding Father Ho Lung of Hurricane Charlie that had struck the island with such devastating and deadly force in the summer of 1951, when he was a child. Hurricane Gilbert was a category 5 storm, one of the largest on record. As winds reached 175 miles an hour, the poorly constructed homes in the ghetto were literally blown away. About eighty per cent of the island's homes were badly damaged and half a million people, a quarter of the population, were made homeless. More than two hundred people were killed. Father Ho Lung's "Diary" entry offers a graphic and

stark description of the hurricane, and the role of the Brothers
in serving the poor in its wake.

> Our gate was flung open as if by the hands of a
> mighty giant. It jammed, and we could not close it
> back; each time we tried, Hurricane Gilbert flung
> us back. Outside our gate the ghetto youths were
> roaming the streets in packs, charged with excite-
> ment, breaking into stores, looting and running
> with packages. Occasionally, we heard a series of
> gunshots, shouting, and screaming, but there was
> also much laughing.
>
> The wildness of the hurricane was bacchanal,
> arousing turbulent emotions. Lawlessness and
> carousing seemed to take control of the blood of
> the ghetto youth. People danced in the rain and the
> wind with wild abandon. They enjoyed the danger
> of the menacing hurricane and seemed to dare it.
> This dangerous mood pervaded the ghetto during
> the storm. I found it strange and disturbing, no less
> so than the mood of Hurricane Gilbert itself.
>
> Practically speaking, I also feared that Faith
> Centre would be invaded by gunmen. That mob
> psychology, looting, and shooting might be brought
> through our iron gate thrown back by the storm.
> During those most terrifying twenty-four hours
> from midnight Sunday to midnight Monday, that
> gate was like the open mouth of a river. But no gun-
> man, no thief came in, only the old, the blind, the
> crippled, the helpless came. Some were lifted up
> bodily by young people in the slums; some walked
> on the arms of others.
>
> The Brothers stayed round-the-clock at Jacob's
> Well and Faith Centre during the hurricane week.

Except for brief sleep they never stopped working. Such generosity! Together with people of the ghetto who work and volunteer all year long, the Brothers dealt solemnly but effectively with the mothers, their children, old folks, and all types of people who were struck severely by Hurricane Gilbert.

Person after person came in. Crowds of people were stuffed onto bed after improvised bed. . . . Food, cocoa, biscuits were organized into the hands of our refugees. Here and there candles were lit, and prayers were said.

Fifteen women packed up food and cooked and never stopped. Pearl, head of them all, kept the pot boiling for seventy-two hours until I ordered her home. The Brothers moved out into the ghettoes and climbed roofs. I don't know how many people's lives touched ours that week. I only know that God moved through the hearts of our Brothers, our workers, and volunteers. Each one worked with a driving grace that could only have come from God alone.[1]

The aftermath of Hurricane Gilbert was as destructive as the violence of the storm itself, laying waste to the lives of those thousands of people who had lost everything in its rage. Father Ho Lung tells the story of one family's loss, a story so powerful and so heart-wrenching that it needs to be told in full:

Hurricane Gilbert bulldozed hundreds of thousands of poor Jamaicans. I don't know how the relief will get to those who are homeless, and by this time, forty days later, there are many for whom the hurricane is a direct road to the madhouse.

---

1. Ibid., 133–34.

Ronald Henry came to me, "Father, I have been walking on the road ever since the hurricane. My house blew down. It wasn't mine, and the landlord said I had to leave, he needed the space now. So I left the one room with Marcia, my wife, and the three children."

I looked at the baby. It was fast asleep in his arms, but it was thin and discoloured, grey rather than black in colour. Marcia stood in the background, her face drawn and thin; and two little kiddies, a little boy and girl, stood by her sucking their fingers, and with big hungry eyes and skinny little limbs.

"I've slept on the roadside and under bus sheds for six weeks. I'm going off my head, Father. If it was I alone, I wouldn't worry. But my wife and little children."

It was a situation that made me feel helpless and somewhat confused. Kingston is so overcrowded and lacking in dwellings. What could I tell this good man? He is devoted to his wife and children and has a job. In days past, people would have taken him in, somehow. They would have squeezed him in. But the ghetto yards are piled up, shack upon shack, with men, with mothers and children, and next door, aunties and uncles and other distant relatives. No one can find a room in the ghetto; there is no space in the yard to build yet another shack, but the people keep piling in.

"Ronald, why don't you go to the country?"

"No one there, Father."

"No relatives in Kingston?"

"No, Father."

"None of your wife's relatives are around?"

"No space, Father."

I called the family together and looked at their faces. They were solemn and speechless. It was as if they were defeated: no smiles, no life, no hope. It was disturbing. They seemed like the Holy Family—Jesus, Mary, and Joseph—and there was no room in the inn.

"I have no room here, not even temporary shelter, Ronald."

"Where can we go?"

There was nothing practical I could do. This vexed me. I could only try to turn their minds to the star of Bethlehem. "Keep looking. You must find a place. If you don't, come back and at least put your head down on the floor of our chapel."

We gave them a little soup. I blessed them, and they went. "Remember, come back if you must. Don't sleep on the sidewalk with the children."

They did not come back. But their haggard and defeated faces come back to me. Where are they now? Will they just add to the number of street people we see throughout Kingston? Will they go mad? Will the children stray like dogs on the street? The numbers of our homeless will increase, not due to Hurricane Gilbert alone, but because we have not heard the cry of the poor. They need to be attended to; they are like children without parents, lost in the wilderness of a mixed-up and confused society. If their hearts stop beating and our eyes are dry, without tears, our hearts will also stop beating. We will still be breathing, but love will have died and so will we.[2]

In October 1988, barely as the dust had settled on the debris

---

2. Ibid., pp. 137–39.

of the previous month's storm, Father Ho Lung was excited to preside over the first ever wedding at Faith Centre. The bride and groom had met through their volunteer work with the Brothers. In their focus on God and His poor they had inadvertently discovered each other.

It says something of the sort of people who lay down their lives to work with the Brothers of the Poor that they should choose to be married in the ramshackle surroundings of a center for the poorest of the poor in the heart of the ghetto, especially as Faith Centre was even more ramshackle than usual in the wake of the hurricane. Father Ho Lung's "Diary" description of the joyful day sets the quixotically delightful scene:

> Cathy and Mike are getting married. All kinds of excitement. The Down's syndrome residents are cleaning the chapel: they are bouncing and chatting away in their special language. Frankie is doing a balancing act with chairs on his head! But his pants are falling off so he has to reach down to pull them—OOPS! Down come the chairs. Wayne is wheeling around the bucket with the mop in it and singing his monotone love song. Harold, lazy as ever, is standing around, arms folded as if he is some supervisor giving orders. He winks at me as I go over and tell Ricky and Dwane how to pack the chairs. When I tell him to work he shakes my hand. You can't win! . . .
>
> Our chapel is used for a night shelter and since the hurricane it has been housing other homeless people as well. Beds, bed pans, walking sticks, clothes had to be moved out. Then we had to decorate with secondhand clothes all these homeless people fit for a wedding.

The chapel was transformed with balloons, streamers, flowers. Our homeless residents, our church people, our ghetto women and men were the invited guests. Then there were the parents of the bride and groom who came from Canada and the United States. Also our local volunteers.

What a marvelous thing! Blacks, Whites, Chinese, Indians, young and old, beggars, professional men and women, the broken, the healthy: all united in this joyous event. The music was lustily sung by all. Deaf and dumb Carl had a great big grin on his face during the whole service, as if he heard the music . . .

What an amalgamation of people God congregates. He seems to me an off-beat God, full of surprises, full of mystery. God draws us to Himself in the poor and binds us together in the Cross. This is our joy![3]

The joy and the brightness of the wedding is all the more incredible in juxtaposition with one of Father Ho Lung's descriptions of the ghetto:

The personality of the ghetto roads and yards exuded waste: the youths and the adults slouched on sidewalks, half-asleep, idly chatting, hanging loose in bars, dulled by music sound systems and sedated by alcohol and drugs. Not even the hagglers and market women seemed intent on sales, and the john crows glided and landed without energy on old dumps and garbage heaps gone stale. Skinny dogs with skeleton ribs and patches of mange walked sniffling the bilge water that lazily ran along

3. Ibid., pp. 93–96.

the side-street gutters. Circling slowly on bicycles
some youths inertly pulled on spliffs and cigarettes
behind dark glasses. The ghetto seemed as languid
as mindless matter.

In the midst of the mindless miasma of the ghetto, there
lumbers Winston, a noble colossus amongst the ghetto's moral
pigmies: "Winston strides bare-backed, sweat gleaming black
in the hot noonday sun. This son of the ghetto is a tall prince,
powerfully built with square shoulders and slim hips. He never
wears a shirt or a smile, or shoes, but only old cut-off trousers.
In the street Winston strolls upright, cool and easy, in full possession of himself, without haste, neither turning to the left nor
the right, his head—the crown of his body—lifted high and dig-
nified." Winston leads Father Ho Lung to his home, a two-room
shack, badly damaged and its contents strewn in complete confusion. He and his family had become the victims of "cocaine
invaders," whom Father Ho Lung describes as "creatures of the
night," who had ransacked Winston's home to feed their drug
habit on the spoils of their ill-gotten gains. He explains to the
priest that he had taken two years to build his home but it had
taken only a few moments for the pillagers to destroy it. He tells
Father Ho Lung it is as though an evil spirit had come from the
belly of the earth to steal everything away. This was his castle,
he explained, built for his "baby mother," i.e., his common law
wife, and their four children. He is most upset by the loss of the
tools of his trade, the means by which he eked a living out of
the economic desert of the ghetto. He is not a beggar; he will
rebuild everything with his own hands. He hopes Father Ho
Lung can help him replace his lost tools. He then philosophizes
about the pitiful state into which the ghetto has plunged, utter-
ing words of wisdom that are not negated by the ghetto patois:

"In time past, people poor because them have no employment. Now them poor because them unemployable. This is a different generation born of the seed of the dragon. The dragon in the book of Revelation now a new idea in poor people's brains. My people used to think, 'I poor but I must be good.' Now them think, 'I poor and I can be badder than the rest.'"

Winston's resilience and his philosophy prompted Father Ho Lung to philosophize along the same lines himself: "This island is spoiled like a blighted mango. We are a young nation, but we are force-ripened by the single controlling thought of sharing the big apple: the American dream. It is weird, odd, out of order, impossible, and finally destructive."[4]

Amidst all the darkness of the ghetto, and the anger and frustration it engendered, Father Ho Lung never fell into despair. On the contrary, hope was always in his heart and laughter on his lips. This overflowing hope and joy appears in his music and in his exuding humor, displayed here in the riotous and rambunctious (and even shocking) humor of one of his "Diary" entries about Desmond, an autistic resident of Faith Centre:

> Desmond's arm, no shorter than a broomstick, reached through the louvers and picked up the two blackie mangoes on my plate. I was startled. Then off he bounded with a big grin upon his face. Everybody laughed. Desmond, who nobody thought was capable of doing anything.

Desmond was so severely autistic, failing to communicate with anyone either by language or by sign, that it was a delightful surprise to discover him capable of such apparent mischief. This episode, however, paled by comparison with his unscheduled appearance during Mass one Sunday. Father Ho Lung had

---

4. Ibid., pp. 100–103.

just given a suitably serious homily on the importance of the
Cross, and Father Hayden, the celebrant, was continuing with
the liturgy. Father Ho Lung takes up the story:

> Then came the most serious part of the Mass: the
> solemn consecration of the bread and wine into the
> body and blood of Christ. Father Hayden lifted the
> host; the bells rang: "*This is my Body.*"
>
> As if from out of nowhere, in ran Desmond,
> stark naked before the altar, with his clothes neatly
> compiled in his hands. His long arms and legs made
> him look like a kangaroo. One of our other resi-
> dents chased after him and quickly ushered him to
> the dormitory. We couldn't subdue our laughter. If
> that wasn't a moment only that master of humour,
> God Himself, could have planned!
>
> Desmond is untrained, and every now and then
> does something socially awkward. Yesterday, he
> chose my fish pond to sit by and rock back and
> forth. When he wanted to pee, he simply turned
> sideways, pulled out his teapot and peed right into
> the fish pond. My poor gold fish must have been
> shocked by the assault of a strange new substance.
> A few may have given up the ghost. Desmond rolled
> over and continued to bask in the sun. . . .
>
> Desmond is autistic. Poor Relief brought him
> here. He was terrified of people. Anytime someone
> drew near, he covered his head with his hands as if
> he was going to be struck. . . .
>
> But he is here now. Little did we know when we
> took him in that he would become so valuable to
> us. What a delight it is to see growth in these for-
> gotten ones. Sonia, one of our workers, chases him
> around the grounds and tickles him. Desmond

laughs uproariously. Wayne helps to dress him and takes him to prayer. Pearl sits down and makes sign language to him. Desmond loves it all.

Today we measure human life according to its productivity. If only we could understand the beauty and value of life for itself and in itself. Desmond is indeed a jewel, but we cannot measure him in terms of dollars and cents. He is just meant to be, and for us it is a matter of being filled with wonder and awe at God's rainbow world, so different, so interesting. There is laughter also, at the foot of the Cross, once we see the world through the eyes of the Maker Himself.[5]

This story was no doubt shocking to many who read Ho Lung's newspaper column and is doubtless shocking to some readers of this biography. Is the most sacred part of the most sacred ritual known to man a subject for jest? If so, are we saying that nothing is sacred? On the other hand, the moment was an epiphanous shining forth of God's providence. As Father Ho Lung expressed it, let's try to see the incident "through the eyes of the Maker Himself." At the consecration, the Body of the Crucified Christ is held aloft for all to see. "This is My Body," says the priest acting *in persona Christi*. And here we see the broken body and mind of a poor creature, made in God's own image but broken, manifesting itself in its naked grotesqueness. In this moment the grotesqueness of Desmond is united with the grotesqueness of the lepers and the men possessed by devils whom Jesus healed; and at the same time the autistic, the possessed, and the leper are transfigured into the grotesqueness of the bruised and bloody Body of Christ Crucified, lifted up for

5. Ibid., pp. 159–61.

all to see so that we may be lifted up with Him. Seen providentially, seen through the eyes of the Maker Himself, this is a miracle being performed for us, a moment of astonishing beauty, which should make us all laugh with sheer joy at the Presence of a loving and self-sacrificial God.

At this juncture, let us pause and ponder the inextricable connection between humor and humility. Indeed there is a connection between Father Ho Lung's seemingly shocking assertion that there is laughter at the foot of the Cross and Chesterton's belief that grotesqueness in nature shone forth the "laughter on the secret face of God." Like Desmond, Chesterton also made use of a fish pond though it must be conceded that he did not use it in exactly the same fashion. He peered rather than peed into the pond and was inspired by the sheer grotesqueness of the fish to see something of God's humor at work.

> For I saw that finny goblin
> Hidden in the abyss untrod;
> And I knew there can be laughter
> On the secret face of God.

Similarly, in his novel *The Man Who was Thursday,* Chesterton, through the character of Syme, mused on the grotesque absurdities of nature, seeing them as God's gargoyles on the cathedral of Creation:

> Syme felt a glaring panorama of the strange animals
> in the cages which they passed. . . . He remembered
> especially seeing pelicans, with their preposterous,
> pendent throats. He wondered why the pelican was
> a symbol of charity, except it was that it wanted a
> good deal of charity to admire a pelican. He remembered a hornbill, which was simply a huge yellow
> beak with a small bird tied on behind it. The whole

gave him a sensation, the vividness of which he
could not explain, that Nature was always making
quite mysterious jokes.[6]

Chesterton knew, as Father Ho Lung knows, that it is not
Nature which makes the jokes but the God of Nature. Indeed
we only have a sense of humor because God shared His sense
of humor with us. Humor is one of the indelible marks of God's
image in us, like love and reason. Animals don't tell jokes, nor
do they laugh.

The reason that God can laugh at great evil is because He is
omnipresent. Everything in time is present to God. There is no
past or future for God. He knows the consequences of Adam's
fall. The Cross is present to God even at the moment that the
serpent is with Eve in the Garden. Creation, Fall, Incarnation,
Crucifixion, Resurrection, Apocalypse: they are always in the
present moment for God. As such, God is no more threatened
by the apparent success of the serpent in the Garden than He is
by the rants of atheists like Richard Dawkins. If parents who are
miserable sinners have to turn their backs on their two-year-
olds after having chastised them, so that the erring child does
not see them laughing, how much more will the loving Father
of Mankind be ultimately amused by the follies of His children?
Sin is serious, to be sure, as serious as the consecration at the
Mass, but only a Puritan or a Pharisee believes that we cannot
laugh about the serious things.

Ultimately the secret laughter on the face of God is the secret
of the joy and mirth in Father Ho Lung and the Missionaries
of the Poor. It is the reason that their motto is "joyful service
with Christ on the Cross." There is humor at the heart of the

6. G. K. Chesterton, *The Man Who Was Thursday*, London: Penguin
Books, 1937, p. 160.

paradox. We can be happy and joyful, and we can laugh, even whilst serving those who suffer great pain.

Where there is joy, there is laughter, even in—especially in—the face of adversity.

One can only make sense of the darkness of evil by seeing it with the light of faith. It is only by seeing in the very midst of human tragedy the presence of the divine comedy that we can be heartened by the knowledge that history, which is His story, has, like all good stories, a happy ending. *There is laughter also, at the foot of the Cross, once we see the world through the eyes of the Maker Himself.*

Chapter Twelve

MISSIONARY PRIEST

IN 1989, a journalist visited Father Ho Lung at Jacob's Well, documenting his and the Brothers' work with the poor: "As we sit, a group of mentally retarded youths stand and stare at us. Another mentally unstable youth passes by. He stares and grins regularly without cause. He comes right up close, almost kisses our faces. He is not the cleanest youth around. He then gently places his hand in Ho Lung's, looks affectionately at him while Ho Lung returns the gesture, squeezing his hand affirmatively. 'Father, I love you,' says the boy."[1]

The journalist listed the achievements of the Brothers of the Poor in the eight years since its founding. Apart from the two centers, which offered residential care for the destitute and disabled, there was a high school for around forty children who would otherwise be too poor to attend school. Some of these had passed their exams with distinction and Father Ho Lung did his best to ensure that they found employment when they left. There were the soup kitchens which fed 550 people, and the food line where two hundred families queued weekly for supplies of food. There was a clothes line and even a shower line where people came just to get a shower. There was also

---

1. *The Jamaican*, 14th edition, 1989.

a health clinic where all the services, including the medicine, were absolutely free. Father Ho Lung insisted that his policy was that everything is free. "We don't charge a cent for anything. Just this week a man came from New York and asked us to take someone he knew. He offered to pay us monthly and I said no, even though he can afford it. Once you start accepting money, you can end up in a situation where those who get in are the ones with the money and the really destitute get left behind."[2]

In spite of these achievements, Father Ho Lung was not resting on his laurels. "I feel that I have achieved so little. I would like to do so much more. I feel I have not learnt to give enough." He referred to a lazy, reluctant part of his character. "I feel that I am not achieving enough for the Lord." He also confessed that he was haunted by the presence of the poor and that he could not be happy unless he was helping them. "I decided that I would never be happy and never have a free conscience if I just had a parish or was involved with scholastics. I had to be with those who were hurting. It is something that haunts me. I knew I would be a very unhappy priest not helping the poor."[3]

Although the Brothers had not yet adopted the white habits with which they are now associated, much of the rigorous daily routine of prayer and service was already in place. Father Ho Lung and the Brothers rose at 5:30 in the morning, beginning the day with Mass and silent prayer. After a long day of service in the centers or in the ghetto, the Brothers returned by 5pm for a further one and a half hours of prayer and meditation based on the spiritual exercises of St. Ignatius Loyola. They slept on bunk beds in communal dormitories and abstained

---

2. Ibid.
3. Ibid.

permanently from smoking and alcoholic beverages. There was no television or other worldly distractions at their residence.

The journalist asked Father Ho Lung whether "the denial of his sexuality" caused him problems and seemed surprised that the priest fielded the question without blushing. "It's hard to describe this unity with God, this love of God which is all-encompassing. You're in love with God. You want nothing. Of course, you do get sexual desires, but you say, cho."[4] He flashed "an enchanting smile" at the journalist and continued. "I treasure my freedom from marriage. If I had a wife I would have to worry about buying a house in upper St. Andrew and seeing that the kids go to elite schools. I wouldn't have the time to give myself totally to the poor. I want a life to take everything out of me. Last night I could not fall asleep because I felt so excited about the prospects of opening a home in Haiti. It's really hard to describe this experience of being in love with God, but I want to leave something for the Lord. I want my life to testify that He is alive."

The journalist, who described himself as "hard-nosed" and "cynical" and who would later embrace the new atheism and sneer at all religion, was nonetheless disarmed by the charm and charisma of this man of faith. "Why don't I feel skeptical about this man's saintly statements? Because there is an avalanche of solid evidence from his life that he means every word. I bid him goodbye. I really want to embrace him but then I would have lost my determined, two-hour struggle to hold back the tears. I am a hard-nosed cynical journalist who has been covering religious personalities for over twelve years. But cynicism simply evaporates in the presence of Richard Ho Lung."[5]

---

4. "Cho" is Jamaican slang. It's an exclamation signifying impatience, scorn, skepticism, or the like.
5. Ibid.

Although the Missionaries of the Poor lead lives of poverty, chastity, and obedience, no one, even in the religious life, is immune to the temptations of the flesh. Father Ho Lung and the leadership of the MOP have occasionally had to confront over the years instances of sexual sin within the community, as is to be expected in any large undertaking, including those inspired by grace. Jesus warns his disciples in *Matthew* 18:7 that occasions of sin are inevitable. But when there has been sin, Father Ho Lung has taken the appropriate steps to reprimand the offenders and, if necessary, exclude them from the community.

In spite of the Founder's charisma and charm, and his proven track record with the poor, the Brothers had been struggling to attract vocations. In 1988, seven years after their founding, there were still only nine brothers, only three more than when they had started. Three of the original Brothers had left, to be replaced by six new vocations, an average of less than one a year. Jamaica's small population, of which less than five per cent were Catholics, could not provide the vocations needed. Inspired perhaps by his meeting with Mother Teresa and his knowledge of her enormous success in attracting vocations in India, Father Ho Lung decided that he would need to look further afield for the vocations he desired. His hope was to build the order to about seventy brothers and to open a center in Haiti in addition to the centers in Jamaica. In retrospect, we can see that his hopes would be exceeded manifold with hundreds of brothers in several countries, spanning across three continents. In the late 1980s, however, even the desire for dozens of Brothers seemed highly ambitious.

In 1987, in order to solve what appeared to be an insurmountable problem, Father Ho Lung made his first visit to India in pursuit of new vocations. "We went to India, to Madras and to

Pondicherry," explains Father Hayden, "because we were told that India had many vocations, enough to export." In India, Father Ho Lung discovered "an immense and vast poverty that [he] had never before imagined or seen."[6]

> There is little water, little food. But the people take care of everything; nothing is thrown out. Everything is carefully used: paper is recycled, drain water is caught and reused. The cold floor and sidewalks, rather than mattresses, are used for sleeping. Every object is a precious gift from God. Most important: every person, no matter how poor, is well regarded. . . .
>
> These people are materially poor, much poorer than the poor of Jamaica; but they are spiritually rich, wealthier than materially rich families who are not spawned in love and not given care. Husbands, wives, and children need to be in each other's arms, giving one another to each other, rather than giving things as a substitute for their presence to each other. We are meant to be a holy Family like Joseph, Mary, and Jesus: brought up in love with a deep and profound respect for God and for one another.[7]

The new strategy of attracting vocations from India paid dividends. By March 1989 there were fourteen Brothers, six of whom were from India. By December, the number of Brothers had risen to seventeen.

In December a journalist from the *Weekend Star* followed Father Ho Lung in his daily work in the Kingston ghetto:

---

6. Ho Lung, *Diary of a Ghetto Priest*, p. 153.
7. Ibid., pp. 153–4.

> The crowd of school children gathered on the cor-
> ner of Laws Street was not alone. In their midst
> was perhaps the most popular, most respected man
> known to them in their community.
>
> The graying hair of Father Richard Ho Lung
> stands out among all others and they were listening
> intently to what he was saying.
>
> In his hand Father Ho Lung held a knife. It was
> taken from a ten-year-old girl who was threaten-
> ing to "stab up" a younger girl. As usual the Ghetto
> Priest, as he is styled, was summoned. He, naturally,
> intervened.[8]

"This incident," the journalist explained, "is similar to many others that Father Ho Lung encounters as he does his evening street walking." She observed him approach two teenage prostitutes, no older than fifteen, speaking to them gently. At this time of year, the priest explained, the Brothers do a lot of house visiting. "We visit the gunmen, the prostitutes and the drug dealers. We win some and we lose some but our message is the same. We tell them about love." That December, the Brothers hosted a party for four hundred children a few days before Christmas and another party for the residents of their centers on Christmas Day.

In July 1990, Cardinal Arinze, then-President of the Pontifical Council for Interreligious Dialogue, arrived in Jamaica on an official visit. It seemed that he was visiting as Pope John Paul II's personal emissary, conveying greetings from the Holy Father at each of his official engagements. In retrospect, it seems that, his visit was intended as a fact-finding exercise on the Pope's behalf, paving the way for John Paul's

---

8. *Weekly Star*, December 15, 1989.

own visit to Jamaica three years later. One imagines that it was Cardinal Arinze's report to him about the visit that first brought the work of the Brothers of the Poor to the Pope's attention. Although Arinze visited several missions, including those run by the Missionaries of Charity and the Mercy Sisters, his visit to Faith Centre was the centerpiece of his time in Jamaica and dominated the media coverage. On July 11, the Cardinal began his day with the Brothers of the Poor by celebrating their regular 6am Mass and then had breakfast with them. After breakfast he went to the studios of the Jamaica Broadcasting Corporation to be interviewed for national television, after which he rejoined the Brothers at Faith Centre. In the coverage of the Cardinal's visit in the *Catholic Reporter* all four photographs focused on his time with the Brothers, including photographs of his celebrating of the Brothers' Mass, his being shown around Faith Centre by Father Hayden, his visiting with those who work at the centre, and his blessing of a crippled resident.

Having been honored by the Church with the visit of the Cardinal, the Brothers received a further honor in October when Jamaica's Governor General, Sir Florizel Glasspole, awarded Father Ho Lung the Order of Distinction "for services to religion and the social welfare of indigents."[9] In the following year, perhaps as a direct result of Carinal Arinze's visit, he received the prestigious Pro Ecclesia et Pontifice Award from the Pope.

Away from the limelight the Brothers continued their work with the poor, particularly with the many street people who had been homeless since Hurricane Gilbert two years earlier. They heard horrific stories of how homeless women were regularly raped, not merely by the dregs of society but by wealthy

---

9. Unidentified newspaper cutting, October 16, 1990.

Jamaicans, so-called "white collar rapists," who travelled the streets in expensive cars looking for victims to abduct. The hapless and helpless women were driven to quiet spots where they were raped and sodomized. One woman claimed to have been sexually molested by up to ten men on more than one occasion. The Brothers took some of the most vulnerable of the homeless to Faith Centre and Jacob's Well, but both centers were full to capacity. Plans were being made to open a new center specifically for the homeless.

Much needed financial assistance arrived in November with the announcement that the Eagle Group of Companies, which employed five hundred people in Jamaica, had initiated a plan whereby each of its employees would be encouraged to contribute $20 a month from their salaries, with the company matching that sum for every contributing employee. The company hoped that this would raise $240,000 a year in financial aid for the Brothers of the Poor. Father Ho Lung was delighted as this was exactly the sort of proactive involvement by Jamaica's businesses for which he had long advocated.

Prompted by the plight of the street people and provoked perhaps by the lack of any adequate response by the government, and buoyed too, no doubt, by the knowledge of extra funds forthcoming from the new business initiative, Father Ho Lung announced in late November that he would be opening a new center for the homeless in the Kingston ghetto. Ironically and perversely, his plans were hampered by Easton Douglas, Jamaica's Minister of Health, who rejected Father Ho Lung's plans for the building. In typically defiant fashion, Father Ho Lung insisted that he would open the center anyway. Raising the ante, he announced that the needs of the street people were so pressing that he would allow the first of them to move in immediately, even while the work on the building was being done. It was as though he was daring the government to be seen to evict the homeless from their only place of refuge. Not for the first time, his courageous stand-off with heartless politicians led to a victory for the poor. Government opposition evaporated and the renovation of the building continued. This third center, which the Brothers named Good Shepherd, was designed to accommodate forty homeless residents but was soon bursting at the seams with almost twice that number, most of whom were elderly, disabled, or otherwise vulnerable. Meanwhile, the chapel at Faith Centre was still being used as a night shelter for the homeless, with people sleeping on mattresses sandwiched between the rows of pews. The recreation area at Faith Centre had been turned into a dormitory, and Jacob's Well was full to bursting with both permanent residents and the street people who arrived each night to sleep.

A few days before Christmas 1990, it was announced that the Brothers would be moving from the overcrowded house on Munroe Street, in which they had resided since 1981, to a new custom-built "monastic"[10] residence in the heart of the ghetto, very close to their three centers for the poor. The move to the ghetto was the fulfillment of Father Ho Lung's desire to live in closer proximity to the poor whom he served. Corpus Christi, as the BOP's new home would be christened, would be an oasis in the urban desert. It contained four dormitories, capable of accommodating up to eighty Brothers, a library, classrooms, a workshop, a kitchen and dining area, restrooms, and a room for recreation or "fellowship." Set on two acres, Father Ho Lung hoped that Corpus Christi could become self-sufficient. The property already contained a number of banana and coconut

---

10. Although the Brothers refer to their religious houses as "monasteries" this is technically a misnomer because the Brothers are not monks but religious Brothers.

trees and a vegetable garden was being prepared and planted. The property also had its own well, ensuring a fresh water supply. Plans were afoot to nourish the spirit as well as the flesh. There would be a chapel at the heart of the complex, and a large rose garden and cloistered area would supply an environment conducive to prayer and meditation.

Corpus Christi opened in the spring of the following year and is still home to many of the Brothers, though Prince of Peace, another "monastic" complex across the road, opened in 1999, is home to many others. Although the hopes of self-sufficiency have not materialized, due in large part to the huge increase in vocations that Father Ho Lung could not have visualized at the end of 1990, the two complexes now have goats and chickens as well as vegetable gardens and fruit trees. Up in the mountains, at a retreat center, which opened in 2004, there is a small farm at which pigs, chickens, and rabbits are raised.

The renovation of Good Shepherd continued in the early months of 1991 and was bolstered in March by the arrival of more than thirty Mennonite men from Kidron, Ohio, who had paid their own air fare to help Father Ho Lung finish the work on the new center. Donating their skills, their time, and the building materials, these men installed toilets, erected partitions and built a dining room during their two weeks of free service to Jamaica's poor.

In July, the Brothers rescued a mentally retarded girl from the streets after she had been raped by three men. In the same week they discovered an old man, Jeremiah Brown, reduced to nothing but skin and skeleton, crawling on the streets like a dog and drinking water from the gutter. He wept when the Brothers picked him up. His children, who now lived in England and the United States, had long since abandoned him. He was taken to Jacob's Well but the ravages of starvation had taken such a toll that he only survived a few days. Brother Max remained with him day and night during his final days. "Thank you son," were the last words he spoke to Brother Max, moments before closing his eyes for the last time.

Although this malnourished man, neglected by his family and neighbors, was an exceptionally heart-wrenching example of the suffering with which the Brothers lived on a daily basis, a litany of others who had died in their care during the previous four weeks serves as a reminder of the lives and deaths of those whom the Brothers have served for over thirty years. Noel Mattison, 72, died of cancer; born a cripple, he was raised in a Catholic orphanage, spent some time on the streets, moved to Eventide and then, finally, to Faith Centre. Hugh Murdock, 70, was blind and had been found on the street with no one to care for him. Patrick Black, described as "a very quiet man," was found with sores all over his body and severely dehydrated due to malnutrition; like Jeremiah Brown he was a pitiful skeletal figure when he died. Carlton Brown was only about thirty when he died; he was blind and crippled and had lost the will to live. Egbert Ellington, 74, also blind and crippled, was living under a tree when the Brothers took him in. Ruby Phillips, 81, had sought help from the Brothers when her house burned down. Vincent Scott, 92, had lost a leg when it was caught in a machine on which he was working and was homeless when the Brothers found him; he lived a full life at Faith Centre, spending the days praying for the poor of Jamaica and for the Brothers of the Poor. After the Brothers had held funeral services for each of these residents of the centers they were taken to the paupers' lot at local cemeteries for burial.

*   *   *

By the end of 1991, there were twenty-two Brothers, five more than at the start of the year. Clearly the strategy of seeking vocations further afield than Jamaica was paying dividends. There were, however, difficulties. Since their first visit to India in 1987, Father Ho Lung or Father Hayden had returned every year. Father Hayden returned in 1988 and Father Ho Lung in 1989 and 1990. Soon Father Ho Lung began to think that these regular visits were not sustainable. "He realized that it was not feasible to keep going and coming from India for two weeks, three weeks, one month," explains Father Hayden.

> The Indian boys wouldn't know us that well. It was very risky and very costly to bring boys all the way from India to Jamaica just on a first encounter without their knowing our character. Many did not stay, most left, most went back, some immediately, some in the long run. Moreover, Father also felt that there was a need to establish a presence in India and for us to become more missionary and not merely Jamaica-based. We had been based in Jamaica for the first ten years as the Brothers of the Poor, but at the beginning of 1992 we became the Missionaries of the Poor. We became really missionary in every sense of the word.

The change of name coincided with the opening of the Brothers' first overseas mission on February 8, 1992, in the diocese of Warangal in Andhra Pradesh, southern India, about a hundred miles north east of the city of Hyderabad. On the invitation of Bishop Thumma Bala of Warangal, Father Ho Lung sent three Brothers, Father Hayden, Brother Philip, and Brother Felix, to pioneer the mission. They would be joined by many other Brothers over the years, greatly extending the charism and apostolic outreach of the rapidly growing Missionaries of the Poor. Today, the Warangal mission is a thriving complex consisting of Christ the King formation house, which was greatly expanded in 2004, House of Joy residential apostolate opened in 2000, and numerous evangelical and pastoral ministries reaching out to thousands of poor people in the area.

The establishment of the first foreign mission had a huge influence on the number of vocations. "In my eleven years there, around 450 boys joined," states Father Hayden. "Of course not all persevered but in those first years we sent over eighty boys to Jamaica for formation. Again, not all persevered but, at this point, Indian vocations are now probably the second largest after the Filipino vocations."

In 1992, Archbishop Leonardo Z. Legaspi, OP, of Caceres, invited the Missionaries of the Poor to officially establish their second overseas mission in Naga City in the Philippines. Father Brian and Brother Max were selected to pioneer the Filipino mission, arriving in Manila on September 28, 1993, the Feast of San Lorenzo Ruiz, the first Filipino Saint. They proceeded to Naga City, eight hours drive from Manila, and began their ministry among the poorest in the Bicol region. Their preliminary works among the poor consisted of visiting the indigent and poor families in the San Rafael squatter and relocation site, bringing them food, clothing, medicines, companionship and pastoral care. They also visited and catechized the scavengers at the City Dump site in Balatas, providing them with both the corporal and spiritual works of mercy. They visited hospitals, working with the patients at Bicol Medical Center and with the mentally ill inmates at the Regional Mental Hospital in Cadlan, Pili.

Father Hayden speaks of the Philippines as a place of "very

vibrant faith," and soon many Filipinos were being sent to Jamaica for formation. The Philippines has provided the most vocations to the MOP. Today over 40 percent of all professed members of the community are from the Philippines.

The MOP mission in Naga City, which was named Heart of Mercy Mission and dedicated to the Sacred Heart of Jesus, grew tremendously and spawned other missions in Cebu in 2004 and Manila in 2011. Father Brian, one of the founding members of the Brothers, served as the pioneering superior for the first ten years, from 1993 to 2003, overseeing the exponential growth of the MOP's mission in the Philippines.

From these ground-breaking beginnings the Missionaries of the Poor continued to expand, eventually opening missions in Haiti, Uganda, Kenya, Indonesia, and the United States. This was a turning point. The change of name indicated a change of focus that would lead to an explosive growth in the number of vocations and the number of places at which the Missionaries of the Poor could reach out to the world's most vulnerable and impoverished people. By the early 1990s Father Ho Lung, the ghetto priest, had well and truly metamorphosed into the missionary priest.

Chapter Thirteen

....

A HOLY FATHER

A S THE Missionaries of the Poor were celebrating the opening of their first foreign mission in India, the *Star* (a Jamaican newspaper) was celebrating Father Ho Lung and Friends, the musical incarnation of the MOP's ministry. In a February 1992 article, the *Star* praised the "special group of generous and gifted volunteers" who, for twenty years, had been performing to raise funds for the poor. The *Star* quoted Father Ho Lung as saying that, over the years, "there are about three hundred songs that the Lord has inspired me to write."[1] The MOP's music ministry continued to go from strength to strength. Father Ho Lung and Friends had won two consecutive JAMI (Jamaica Music Industry) awards, in 1989 and 1990, for best musical and continued to win awards, year after year. Their shows played to packed houses in Jamaica, as well as in Toronto, Miami, Boston, Detroit, New York, Atlanta, Rhode Island, Trinidad, and Guyana.

The success of the concerts in North America had much to do with a growing army of lay volunteers, the Friends of the Poor, who helped to promote and organize the concerts, as well as to raise money for the MOP missions. By 1992 there were

---

1. Jamaican *Star*, February 25, 1992 .

chapters of the Friends of the Poor in Toronto, Atlanta, and Miami.

On March 3, 1992, Father Ho Lung and Friends again won the JAMI for best musical, this time for their latest show, *Praise Him!*. Father Ho Lung and Friends performed live at the awards ceremony, on the same bill as stars of the Jamaican music scene, such as Ken Boothe, Marcia Griffiths, and Boris Gardner. In early April, Father Ho Lung and his entourage of singers travelled to Canada to perform *Praise Him!* in Toronto.

As the Missionaries of the Poor moved confidently into its second decade of existence, Father Ho Lung's dynamism was at the heart of their charism. In his life and work, he was a brother to the poor of Jamaica, a missionary to the poor of India and the Philippines, and the reggae priest to the thousands of people who came to see him and his "friends" perform.

In August 1993 Father Ho Lung experienced one of the undoubted highlights of his life when John Paul II visited Jamaica. In order to look their best for the Pope it was decided that the Brothers should adopt a conventional white habit, rather than the somewhat casual blue shirts and khaki pants that they'd worn up until that point. Having adopted a new name in the previous year to coincide with the opening of the mission in India, the Missionaries of the Poor now adopted the new habits in honour of the Holy Father's visit.

Father Ho Lung's impressions of the Holy Father were recorded on the Feast of the Assumption (August 15) in an article for the *Sunday Gleaner*:

> He is the greatest spiritual force of our times, and at
> the same time, the warmest and most personable of
> people anyone could meet.

A rastaman at Gold Street threw his arms around John Paul II and gave him a hairy hug; the Pope gave him a warm spontaneous embrace and a big smile.

A fat Jamaican woman emerged from a bar and flung him a hearty embrace; being a big man himself, he matched her great warmth, again with a hug.

He broke the barrier of security and walked along Gold Street, shaking everyone's hands and the hands of the ghetto people whom the security considered to be dangerous. On our violent island and in a violent location he made himself vulnerable, because of love for our poor. . . .

Anti-Catholicism and anti-Vatican sentiments are still in existence in our island. The only way it can be broken is by the language of love in action. This is what John Paul's action said. By being one with the people, loving our brothers and sisters—risking even death—our Pope re-enacted Christ's movement among the poor and forgotten. . . .

All of us must cast aside our fears: like His Holiness, we must be among the poor, we must leave behind the security of our middle and upper class homes. . . .

The Missionaries of the Poor sang their hearts out; we tried to dance too, we shouted, laughed, shoved and pushed like everyone. It was joyous, marvelous. All priests, religious brothers and sisters were elated to meet "Papa." Many held his hands, kissed his ring, looked into his eyes. Every brother was met and given his warm smile and touch. . . .

[W]e talked to each other, he couldn't understand my English, I couldn't understand his Polish or Italian. But the language barrier didn't matter;

through our attempts to communicate there were so many smiles, direct gazes into each other's eyes, hands joined in love.

I walked hand in hand in heaven when at the end of Morning Prayer at the Holy Trinity Cathedral on Tuesday morning, a papal priest asked me to come forward with Sister Loretta, Superior of the Missionaries of Charity. I was surprised and did not know what was happening. . . .

I was confused when I saw Archbishop Samuel Carter, other bishops and a few members of the Papal party beckoning that I was to come forward. I kissed the Pope's ring; he placed a fatherly hand on my head and blessed me, then held my hand, and walked with me hand in hand from the top of the sanctuary where he was seated, to the Blessed Sacrament at the bottom right hand side of the sanctuary.

I was walking in the clouds, in heaven, hand-in-hand with this beautiful Saintly man, our own Pope, John Paul II. I felt his warmth, gentleness and strength in that hand. . . . I am overcome with joy and a deep knowledge of my own unworthiness. I am a very happy Priest; I love the Priesthood and all the sacrifices it requires; I love the Poor, my island, and my beloved brothers.

Brother Max got patted on the cheek; the Holy Father held the head of Brother Steve and prayed over him for a long time; he held hands with so many of our brothers. He . . . offered his hand to our helpers—June, Phylis, Brother Joe, Rena and her friends nearly died with joy.

> The most beautiful of two gestures I witnessed
> close at hand were when he rubbed foreheads and
> laughed beautifully in the face of Donovan, one
> of our residents who cannot walk and is dwarfed
> and shriveled in size. Finally, he knelt and kissed
> the ground before one of our wheelchair residents,
> Charles, who cannot speak or walk. Charles looked
> up to heaven and broke into a magnificent smile
> of joy.[2]

It was singularly apt that Father Ho Lung's memories of the Papal visit, basking in the afterglow of the Holy Father's presence, should have been published on the Feast of the Assumption. It was almost as if the ghetto priest had temporarily been assumed into heaven himself by the experience!

Remembering the Pope's visit to Jamaica almost twenty years later, the enthusiasm and joy seems hardly diminished. "It was like walking on a cloud," he exclaimed, breaking into laughter. "He landed at the airport, and he came immediately to the ghettos. That was it! Straight from the airport to the ghettos! He went to Mother Teresa's home that is close to us, less than a block away from us. I remember he was surrounded by all these police. They were afraid that something might go wrong, because our area is really a violent area. He came and all these policemen were around, and the first thing he did was to break through all that, which I thought was incredible."

He recalled the incidents that had struck him at the time as if it were yesterday: "There was this big black Jamaican woman at the bar, and she stood outside, and she was watching and waving to him. He was trying to reach out and to engage with the people. The police were trying to hold him back. And this

2. *Sunday Gleaner*, August 15, 1993.

woman threw her arms around him, and as she did so she yelled out, *'I am never going to bathe again.'"* Father Ho Lung laughs as he remembers the scene: "'*Never going to bathe again!'* She was so happy. He brought forth happiness and spontaneity."

Father Ho Lung spoke of the joy that the Brothers felt in the Pope's presence: "Our brothers played guitar and sang the Magnificat. They sang and danced and so forth. He met the brothers. He went around and shook their hands." Father Ho Lung then mentioned his own "funny meeting" with the Pope, in which the Pope seemed to be speaking Italian to him, whilst he was speaking English to the Pope. "We didn't really understand each other and yet there was a very deep connection. He was trying so much to engage with me and I was trying to engage with him. He communicated in his warmth that 'we are one,' and that was sufficient for me." It is hard to believe that the Pope would be speaking Italian, or Polish, in an English-speaking country. Perhaps it was their respective dialects, rather than their respective languages, which was the problem. One can imagine the Pope asking Father Ho Lung something in his broad Polish accent and Father Ho Lung replying in his heavy Jamaican brogue and neither being able to understand the other!

Sadly, there was a darker side to the Pope's visit that was glossed over at the time but which Father Ho Lung revealed to me in our discussions. There were some dissenting voices amongst certain Catholics who were not happy at the prospect of the schedule for the papal visit including a visit to Faith Centre. Perhaps they were resentful of the amount of attention that Cardinal Arinze's visit to Faith Centre had received during his visit three years earlier. In any event, they threatened Archbishop Carter that they would boycott the papal Mass at the national stadium if Faith Centre was on the Pope's itinerary. Although the original plans were apparently for the Pope to visit Faith Centre after his visit to the Missionaries of Charity, which would have made sense logistically considering that the two centers are within yards of each other, the Archbishop reluctantly agreed to cancel the visit to the Missionaries of the Poor. He informed Father Ho Lung of the decision, which, in spite of his disappointment, Father Ho Lung accepted for the good of the Church and to maintain the peace.

In spite of the dissenting voices apparently winning the day, Archbishop Carter, who had always been very supportive of the works of the Brothers, found ways of circumventing the efforts to cold-shoulder the Missionaries of the Poor. The Brothers managed to meet the Pope on three separate occasions during his very short visit, which Father Ho Lung attributes to Archbishop Carter. Although this may be true, I can't help but wonder whether Archbishop Carter was also responding to the Pope's own personal insistence that he meet Father Ho Lung. This seems likely considering the central role that the visit to Faith Centre and the celebration of Mass with the Brothers had played in Cardinal Arinze's visit. Isn't it likely that Arinze reported to the Pope about the visit? Isn't it probable, in fact, that Arinze's visit was part of the early planning for the Pope's visit to Jamaica, a reconnaissance mission? This being so, it is clear that the Pope would have received glowing reports of the work that the Brothers were doing with the poor of the ghetto and would have desired to visit Faith Centre, as his emissary Cardinal Arinze had done. It seems likely, therefore, that John Paul II was personally involved in rectifying the sin of omission. His apparently unscheduled call for Father Ho Lung to come forward during Morning Prayer in the cathedral bears all the hallmarks of papal intervention. Whether this is so, Father Ho Lung's memory of the unexpected surprise shone across the years as brightly as ever:

What was very beautiful was at the cathedral when, to my astonishment, while I was kneeling and praying, someone tapped me on the shoulder. I didn't know what was going on. I looked up and he said, "Come." "No," I said, "you have the wrong person." Then he went over to the superior of the Mother Teresa sisters, and he called her up. Then he came back again and told me, "You're to come. Come. Come. Come." I still thought he had the wrong person and I asked him who he was you looking for. Finally he just grabbed me by the hand and said, "Come." I found myself standing before the Pope who was sitting at the main chair for the celebrant. I just looked at him. I didn't know what to do. I didn't know whether I was to kneel or to stand, so I just stood there. The Pope came out of his chair, and he held me by the hand.

After he took my hand he began to walk with me through the cathedral. I felt really as though I was walking in heaven. It was a wonderful, wonderful feeling, and he was so warm. He just held my hand through the entire time, and he looked at me and he smiled at me. People clapped and so forth. I didn't really understand what was going on.

Father Ho Lung discovered later that the person who had sent the usher to summon him was Archbishop (now Cardinal) Dziwisc, the Pope's private secretary and one of his closest friends, a fact that reinforces the likelihood that it was not Archbishop Carter but the Pope himself who was responsible for giving the ghetto priest the biggest and best surprise of his life.

At the papal Mass at the national stadium, the climax and culmination of John Paul II's visit, Father Ho Lung and the

Brothers were assembled with several of the disabled residents from the centers when the Pope again approached. He blessed Father Ho Lung once again and blessed the Brothers, taking their hands. He then knelt down and kissed the feet of a little crippled girl named Sharon, a resident of the centers.

The Pope's visit was very brief. He stayed two nights and only one full day. It was as sudden as a flash of lightning and as powerful. During the brief moment of brilliance, Father Ho Lung had literally had the time of his life, being both humbled and exalted by his experience of the Holy Father's love. As for Blessed John Paul, he was living up to one of his titles as Pope in his love for Ho Lung and the Brothers. He was being the Servant of the servants of God and a servant of the servants of the Poor.

Chapter Fourteen
....

THE BROTHERS
COME OF AGE

IN THE afterglow of John Paul II's visit, Father Ho Lung and the Missionaries of the Poor continued their work in Jamaica, India, and the Philippines.

On November 11, 1993, the Canadian High Commissioner (the top diplomat in Jamaica) visited the Brothers in the Kingston ghetto and handed Father Ho Lung a substantial check from the Canadian International Development Agency to help with the construction of new centers for the destitute. Apart from such donations, the other major source of income for the MOP was the music apostolate. At the end of 1993, Father Ho Lung's latest musical, *Sugar Cain*, was staged at the Little Theatre in Kingston. He described it as "a musical tragedy . . . and archetypal adaptation of the story of Cain and Abel . . . which is reflected in the social relations between so many half-brothers and half-sisters resulting from casual sexual liaisons."[1] In the following June, Father Ho Lung and Friends garnered another JAMI award when *Sugar Cain* won the prize for best musical. Father Ho Lung and his musical collaborator, Jon Williams, won an additional composers' award for "best original music." By the beginning of 1994, Father Ho Lung and

---

1. *Outlook Magazine*, October 10, 1993.

Friends had released twelve albums and had completed more than fifty overseas fundraising tours. Many of those who had seen Father Ho Lung and Friends in concert became lay associates, helping to raise funds for the MOP in their local parishes. Shipments of food and other essentials to Kingston from the United States and Canada increased throughout the 1990s enabling the Brothers to continue the expansion of their ministry in the ghetto.

On January 15, 1994, Father Ho Lung was presented with the Martin Luther King Jr. Humanitarian Award at the Jamaica American Society's annual banquet, held at Kingston's Wyndham Ballroom. This was the latest addition to a lengthening list of awards that he had received over the years, including those presented by Guinness, the *Gleaner* newspaper, the Jamaica Chamber of Commerce, and the City of Miami, not to mention the prestigious Order of Distinction awarded by the Jamaican Governor-General and the even more prestigious Pro Ecclesia et Pontifice Award bestowed upon him three years earlier by the Pope.

At the beginning of 1994, the Missionaries of the Poor was expanding on all fronts. There were now forty Brothers based in Jamaica, India, and the Philippines, and the mission in Haiti, for which Father Ho Lung had long been working and praying, was opened in January. "Father sent two brothers to Haiti," recalled Father Hayden, "to Cap Haitien, the second largest city. We had been going there for years, since the very early days. Brian and I went there for three months of formation with the Missionaries of Charity. So we had a connection to Haiti very early and we got our first two Haitian vocations in 1989. One's still with us, Brother Louima. He's now in the Philippines. It was good to finally establish a permanent presence there. Haiti is still considered the poorest country in the western world."

Brother Louima was one of the two Brothers sent to Cap Haitien to establish the mission, the other being Brother Eugene, a vocation from India. Initially the Haitian mission ran a residence for the homeless and for abandoned elderly people but, as with the MOP missions elsewhere, their apostolate soon expanded to include a home for orphans and disabled children.

In India, under the pioneering leadership of Brother Hayden, the MOP ran a night shelter for the homeless and also fed and cared for fifty lepers. In the Philippines, under the guidance of Brother Brian, the MOP mission ministered to the needs of the slum-dwellers.

Back in Jamaica, construction had begun on Lord's Place, the fourth MOP center in the Kingston ghetto. Set to open in November 1994, it would care for orphans and malnourished and disabled children, the elderly, mentally ill young women, and those terminally ill with AIDS. Today, Lord's Place has more than 150 residents.

Father Ho Lung was now writing two regular newspaper columns, "Diary of a Ghetto Priest" and "Between Good and Evil," both of which had a powerful impact in raising awareness of the plight of Jamaica's poorest people.

Help was now coming from all quarters as people became increasingly aware of the work and needs of the MOP. In May 1994, the US Navy unloaded five hundred mattresses, which it had donated to the Brothers, at Port Royal, Jamaica. Even as the US Navy was delivering its valuable gift to the MOP, Father Ho Lung was in Canada, giving talks at Catholic parishes to raise awareness of his work. In Moorestown, New Jersey, a particularly active group of lay associates of the MOP were raising funds, and individuals in the area had contributed with great generosity. One paid for a supply of crosses and breviaries for the Brothers, another covered the cost of the MOP's annual water bill of $3,000, and a third paid to support a nurse for the Brothers. Such support was crucial to the success of the Brothers' work, supplemented always by the annual musicals in Jamaica, the next of which, *The Rock*, opened at Kingston's Little Theatre on October 7. Based on the life of St. Peter, whom Father Ho Lung described as "frail, simple, weak, undeserving, but who Christ simply loves," the musical's climax was the first Pope's martyrdom. "Despite his sins," Father Ho Lung stated, "Peter was lifted up and made a great disciple, becoming the rock upon which the Church was built. The story shows you how, although encased by a simple nature, God creates great heroes and loves and chooses the humble to do great things for Him."[2] In the spring of 1995, Father Ho Lung and Friends took *The Rock* on the road, playing to packed houses in the United States and Canada. Later in the year, they made their first trip across the Atlantic to England, performing in London, Northampton, and Bedford.

*   *   *

In April 1995, Father Ho Lung became embroiled in a heated debate with members of the Jamaican medical profession who were seeking the legalization of abortion. At a meeting to discuss the issue, Father Ho Lung had raised tension by showing an anti-abortion film as a prelude to the discussion, which depicted the dismembered bodies of aborted babies. Tensions were heightened further by Father Ho Lung's insistence that abortions "were not acceptable under any circumstances." Other Catholic priests in attendance asked the doctors what right they had to kill babies. They insisted that the issue was

---

2. *Outlook Magazine*, October 9, 1994.

purely a moral one and that no pragmatic reasoning could alter that fact. In response to an obstetrician's attempts to rationalize the merits of legalizing abortion, Father Ho Lung interjected angrily, asking the doctor how he could possibly justify his position. "How can you think you have any power over life," he demanded. "You have no right."[3] As tempers flared, all but one of the doctors walked out of the discussion, indicative of the anger and polarization that the issue of abortion would continue to cause in the years ahead.

Medical practice of a different kind was in evidence in September when an American Catholic surgeon operated on Jason, an eight-year-old resident of one of the MOP centers, to remove a grapefruit-sized tumor from his neck and face. Jason was flown to New Jersey for the operation. A local Catholic parish paid for his flight, and the surgeon, Martha Matthews, performed the surgery free of charge.

*   *   *

The twenty-fifth anniversary of Father Ho Lung's ordination was commemorated at a Mass on July 4, 1996, at which the new Archbishop of Kingston, Edgerton Clarke, was the principal celebrant with his predecessor, Archbishop Samuel Carter, concelebrating. Twenty-nine MOP Brothers were present at the silver jubilee Mass. "Twenty-five years ago I was ordained a priest but it was fifteen years ago that I began to live a life of self-sacrifice," Father Ho Lung said in his homily, reminding those present that his twenty-fifth anniversary as a priest also marked the fifteenth anniversary of the Missionaries of the Poor. During the first ten years of his priesthood he had not

---

3. Unidentified newspaper cutting, April 11, 1995.

offered his heart to God, he explained, but from the time of the founding of the Brothers he had been "haunted by the presence of God." He and Fathers Hayden and Brian had been stripped of everything, leaving them with the naked desire to serve God. "God desires that we strip ourselves so he can comfort us and punish us and thrust us into the world for us to do his will."[4] One particular cause for celebration was that the MOP now had seventy Brothers, natives of Jamaica, Trinidad, St. Lucia, Haiti, Belize, Dominica, India and the Philippines, all of whom had answered the same call to strip themselves naked for Christ.

Two years later, on the Feast of the Annunciation in 1998 (March 25), the Missionaries of the Poor reached another milestone when Archbishop Edgerton Clarke erected the MOP as a Religious Institution of Diocesan Right, the first time in the English-speaking Caribbean that a male religious order had been elevated to such a status by the Holy See. During a solemn Mass at Kingston's Holy Trinity Cathedral, the Archbishop read the decree from Rome that declared that "the pattern of life that the Missionaries of the Poor have set down for themselves fully conforms to that way of life understood by the Church to be a life consecrated to God through the profession of the evangelical counsels." In addition to the evangelical counsels of poverty, chastity, and obedience, the Brothers also took a fourth vow of free service to the poor. The additional vow was intended to ensure that the Missionaries of the Poor would always stay unequivocally focused on the needs of the poorest and most needy members of society. In practical terms, it meant that no Brother could have a personal bank account or keep money with him, nor could any Brother start a business intended for profit. Trusting fully in Divine Providence they

---

4. *Catholic Opinion*, August 1996.

would rely on the generosity of fellow Christians to provide for their needs.

Their needs were minimal. Centered on a life of prayer and service, the Brothers possessed only three sets of religious habits (white cassocks, khaki pants, blue or beige shirts, and undergarments), a pair of sandals, a cross, two pairs of work and sports attire, a bible, one spiritual reading book, and their study notes. Each Brother went through six years of formation, including a two year novitiate and a three year juniorate. During their formation, they were taught scripture, Church history, Church documents, literature, nursing, music, ethics, and the rules, history, and spirituality of the MOP. Integral to the training of the Brothers was learning to take care of the poor and sick and learning to live in community and prayer. Clearly, with the total number of Brothers now numbering ninety, with thirty Brothers in the novitiate, and with the Papal recognition of their formal status as a religious order, the Missionaries of the Poor were coming of age.

Chapter Fifteen

....

JOYFUL SERVICE WITH CHRIST ON THE CROSS

THE joyous occasion of the Missionaries of the Poor being raised by the Archbishop to the status of a religious institute was a mark of the MOP's success. It was a confirmation and celebration of the rich fruits of their labors. It was the frosting on the cake. The frosting is, however, not the whole cake, nor is it the largest part or even the most important part of the cake. For Father Ho Lung and the Missionaries of the Poor the most important parts of the cake were the crumbs of comfort that they could offer to the poorest of their brothers and sisters. The cake was to be shared with others, especially with the hungriest. This overarching priority is evident in the MOP's motto, *Servitium Dulce cum Christo Crucifixo* (Joyful Service with Christ on the Cross), which was unveiled at the time of their gaining papal recognition as a religious institute. It is, therefore, appropriate that we turn our attention once more to the MOP's ministry to the poor.

Anyone who has visited the MOP centers has poignant memories of their heart-wrenching and heart-warming experiences with the residents. One such experience was that of Linda Dix. Mrs. Dix, the director of religious education at a parish in

Moorestown, New Jersey, was a regular visitor to the centers in Kingston and remembered witnessing the death of a child.

> Frail Ivonne lay very still in her little lower bunk as around her stood crying all the abandoned children with whom she had lived and played. They had lost one of their own and were heartbroken. Yet they knew enough to kneel as one of the missionary priests came forward to bless their tiny friend. All began to pray the Our Father in a ritual to which they had grown accustomed. As I lifted my head from the prayer, I watched older children from the shelter arrive carrying weeds they had picked. . . . They laid these to rest at Ivonne's feet. The sobs of the children subsided as Father Hayden's comforting words of hope rose above their sadness.
>
> I, too, was overwhelmed with grief for I had come to know and love Ivonne. In April, only three months before, she had been playing and singing beside me in our sunny afternoon jamborees at the mission. Her voice was now part of the heavenly chorus. . . . Father Hayden's words were reassuring. "The child did not die nameless or abandoned but rather she was surrounded by love."[1]

On May 13, 1998, the Brothers received a call informing them that a man was lying in the street in an appalling condition, possibly dying. As they arrived on the scene they were shocked at what they discovered. A young man lay in the gutter, having clearly been neglected by passers-by for several days. His arm was broken in three or four places, the result of shielding his head from blows during a vicious assault, and his head had been eaten away by maggots to such an extent that

---

1. Unidentified press cutting, March 27, 1997.

the whole top of his skull was visible. The stench was overpowering. He was so malnourished that he could quite accurately be described as being nothing but skin and bones. His ragged clothes and body were caked in mud. "He was semi-conscious," explained Father Ho Lung. "He didn't remember who beat him and he was in a bad state."[2] He was taken to Faith Centre, where the brothers fed him with liquid and gave him a shower. They shaved his head and then painstakingly removed each of the hundreds of maggots from his head, an operation that took several hours.

Considering that the man was left in the gutter after being assaulted and was ignored by countless passers-by until the Brothers arrived, it is not surprising that one newspaper described the whole incident as "an uncanny replay of the Biblical story of the Good Samaritan."[3] In this incident, as in countless other instances in the preceding seventeen years, the Missionaries of the Poor were not only good Samaritans but were the veritable presence of Christ in the midst of the ghetto.

Just two weeks after the starving young man with the broken bones and maggot-infested head wound had been brought to Faith Centre, three young men in far happier circumstances arrived. Marcus Gayle, Robbie Earle, and Fitzroy Simpson, three professional soccer players from the English Premier League, visited the residents. The three men were part of the Jamaican national team, affectionately known as the Reggae Boyz, which had made history by being the first team from the English-speaking Caribbean to qualify for the World Cup Finals. The meeting of the Reggae Boyz with the reggae priest was too good a photo opportunity for the media to resist. One

---

2. *Weekend Star*, May 15, 1998.
3. *Sunday Herald*, May 17, 1998.

newspaper published a large photograph of Father Ho Lung
with the three soccer stars and reported that the players were
given "a spiritual send-off" by Father Ho Lung on the eve of
their final warm-up game in the United States before flying to
France for the Finals.[4] In January of the following year, Prince
Michael of Kent became the first member of a royal family to
visit the MOP centers. The meeting of the prince and the paupers offered the media a photo opportunity as enticing as that
between the reggae priest and the Reggae Boyz.

*   *   *

In June 1998, the Jamaican government announced its plans
to transfer forty mentally handicapped adults from one of its
state-run facilities to the care of the Missionaries of the Poor.
The decision represented an endorsement by the government
of the MOP's work and an acceptance of the fact that religious
bodies played a vital role in helping the disabled receive the
care that they needed. Further confirmation of the warming of
relations between the government and the MOP was evident
in the following month when Jamaica's Prime Minister, P. J.
Patterson, visited the centers. Following his visit, he announced
that the government would assist the Missionaries of the Poor
with the payment of their utility bills and promised that the
National Water Commission would upgrade the water supply at Faith Centre and Jacob's Well. The support of the Prime
Minister was a welcome breakthrough in relations between
the MOP and the government, a far cry from the early days in
which Father Ho Lung and the politicians were at loggerheads.
In August, Father Ho Lung claimed that the dramatic

---

4. *Daily Gleaner*, May 30, 1998.

improvement in the health of a two-year-old who was expected
to die within a week of the Brothers taking him in was a miracle
of love. Earlier in the year, when he was admitted to one of the
MOP centers to receive hospice care, the toddler's doctor had
predicted that he would die within a couple of weeks. Seven
months later, against all expectations, little Marrio Myers was
showing great improvement. Marrio had suffered from hydrocephalus since birth, a tragic medical condition which causes
a build-up of fluid in the head, resulting in the head becoming grossly and grotesquely enlarged while the rest of the body
remains under-developed. By the time that Marrio was handed
into the care of the Brothers his head had a circumference of
more than five feet and weighed thirty-five pounds, almost
double the weight of the rest of his body. Unable to lift his head,
he was unable to move. It took three people to move him to prevent the weight of his head from breaking his neck. The pressure of the liquid on the brain also retards the development of
certain functions, such as speech and the movement of limbs.

Asked to explain the mysterious improvement in Marrio's
health, Father Ho Lung attributed it to the love of the people
caring for him. "It has to be love," he said. "I just find love to
be a miraculous potion."[5] He referred especially to the way in
which other residents at the center had responded lovingly
to their new neighbor. "We have found him to be improv-
ing," Father Ho Lung continued. "He is getting taller . . . more
aware." The surprising improvement in Marrio's condition
led some American doctors to bring him to the United States
for a delicate operation to remove the fluid from his head.
The operation took place at the same hospital in New Jersey
at which eight-year-old Jason had been operated upon three

---

5. *The Gleaner*, August 28, 1998.

years earlier. Again, the surgeons offered their services free of charge. "The goodness of people continues to amaze me more and more," said Father Ho Lung, referring not only to the generosity of the surgeons but also to Air Jamaica for flying Marrio to the United States and to the American Embassy for granting Marrio an emergency visa at very short notice. "It is like the Holy Spirit is working to protect life," he added.[6]

A month or so after the operation, Father Ho Lung flew to New Jersey to see Marrio, who was recuperating with a local family. While Ho Lung was there, a journalist visited the house at which Marrio was staying. His record of the encounter illustrates Father Ho Lung's love for the poor and the happiness he derives from it. "When we are motivated by love and a trust in God, marvelous things can happen," Father Ho Lung told the journalist. "The more you sacrifice, the freer you are as a human being. Free from selfishness. I can't think of a happier life. I love to see all these poor people happy that they are being relieved of pain." The subject of conversation turned to Marrio. "His little, little legs and little, little arms are out of proportion, and yet we find him beautiful," said Father Ho Lung, looking at the tiny child in their midst. "This little creature has brought so much joy to our lives."[7] He stroked Marrio's belly gently while the boy was being fed black cherry yogurt. "He likes sweet things," he said, moving his hand to Marrio's cheek. "What an appetite. What an appetite!" The boy hummed as he ate. "That means he's happy," Father Ho Lung added.

Also present was a thirty-two-year-old American, Kim George, who had been born with hydrocephalus and had been operated on forty-eight times by surgeons. "It's just remarkable

---

6. Ibid.
7. Unidentified press cutting, October 25, 1998.

that Marrio has lived this long," she said. She'd asked her neurosurgeon how the child had stayed alive and he told her that he could "only say by the grace of God." Clearly moved by Marrio's case when she'd heard about it in the local newspaper, she regularly drove for forty-five minutes to bring the boy clothes, diaper wipes and toys. "I gave him a Winnie the Pooh because every child should have a Winnie the Pooh," she said. She also had nothing but praise for Father Ho Lung for his role in saving Marrio's life: "God put him on the face of the Earth for a reason—these children need him, that country needs him, everybody needs him. Everybody could use a dose or two of Father Ho Lung."[8]

Returning to Jamaica, Father Ho Lung again spoke of the joy of serving the poor at a meeting of the Kingston Rotary Club in December at which he was awarded the Club's Most Distinguished Citizens Award: "To be at oneness with the poor, the suffering, the blind, the deaf, the widows, the orphans, the crippled, and the old . . . to give and give until we are washed pure of any selfish desire, then to die at the foot of the Cross, and to kneel in a state of nothingness before the Almighty . . . that is what brings happiness."[9]

To be at one with the poorest is to be richer than a king; to suffer with the afflicted is to be healed; to give is to receive; to die is to live; to kneel in a state of nothingness is to rise with the resurrected Christ to the only thing worth anything. To share in the misery of others is the path of true happiness. All of this wisdom was but foolishness to the world. Father Ho Lung, like the Trinity he worships, and the God-Man he serves, is paradox personified, though on a much smaller scale, of course.

---

8. Ibid.
9. Unidentified press cutting, December 1998.

The paradox was exemplified by the choice of Mary, Cause of our Joy, as the patroness of the Missionaries of the Poor. Mary, the seat of wisdom and the mirror of justice, is the happiest woman alive because she leads us to her Son, the happiest Man who ever lived. To be led by Mary to the Crucified Jesus is not merely the only way to live happily, it is the only way to live happily ever after. It was no wonder that Father Ho Lung was always smiling. He had the secret to happiness and wanted to share it with anyone who would listen.

Chapter Sixteen

....

BLOOD ON THE STREETS

Fallen, fallen is Babylon the great! It has become a
dwelling place of demons, a haunt of every foul spirit.
—Revelations 18:2

"GUNMAN a come! Lord God in heaven." Crowds scattered on either side of the street, driven as if a tidal wave had swept down the middle of Heroes Circle. The posse [i.e., criminal gang] strode towards Stephens Street. People screamed and jumped over fences, others fled across Heroes Circle. Down came the vigilantes, full of malice, menacing with guns in hand and in pocket. Their shoulders were high, like those of commanders of armies. They rode through the streets with pride, proclaiming their terrible intentions. . . . They were masters of darkness and death. They had fully imbibed the lessons of the evil one.

Some of these men laughed as they saw the poor people scatter like rabbits. They enjoyed their authority as masters do over servants in a place of wickedness. They reviled their own poor people and the servility imposed by terror. Power, the taste of it, how sweet! Even though they themselves were dispossessed in their own ghetto lives and it was dominance over their own poor, it was delicious. These were the new lords of evil, top ranking kings of darkness, inherited from a politics of retribution in the recent history of our island. . . .

> Roland was in bed. "I tired, I want sleep," he told Mel. "I gwine lay down a little while."
>
> Roland flopped into bed. The little children flopped into bed with him. They loved Roland. Although he was sixteen years old and had big strong shoulders, he was not like other men. He liked little children, and he often lifted them gently on his shoulders or he would whirl them around in a circle faster and faster, till they got dizzy and fell down laughing in ecstasy.
>
> When the gunmen came he was asleep. The little children heard the gun shots and the shouting, but Roland was fast asleep. The mothers and young adults ran into their rooms and grabbed their little children. Little Maisie screamed when her mother was suddenly confronted by seven gunmen. "Get her out of here." One shoved the mother and child aside.
>
> Roland jumped out of sleep and under the bed. "Get out of there." Silence. "I say, get out from under the bed." Silence. They threw the little bed out the door. Then they picked up Roland and slapped him. "Why you don't answer when big man talk to you?" They slapped him again and again. He whimpered. Then the leader placed the gun by his ear and shot him. Little Maisie ran away from her mother and screamed, "Roland." The gang leader kicked her. Maisie flew back to her mother.[1]

---

1. Ho Lung, *Diary of a Ghetto Priest*, pp. 108–109.

At the end of 1998, the MOP published *Diary of a Ghetto Priest*, a collection of some of the best articles that Father Ho Lung had written for his regular newspaper column in the *Gleaner*. Apart from detailing the daily life of the Brothers in their ministry to the poor, Father Ho Lung's "Diary" also highlighted the squalor and violence of daily life in the ghetto, of which this graphic depiction of the terror caused by the ghetto's gunmen was typical.

In April 1999, the Brothers opened Prince of Peace, their second "monastic" residence, which, like their other residence, Corpus Christi, just across the street, was situated in the heart of the ghetto. At its opening, Prince of Peace served as the juniorate home for those Brothers in formation. Today it is home to the fully professed Brothers who have taken their perpetual vows. A few days after the opening of Prince of Peace, Father Kenneth Payne, an English priest and longstanding supporter of the work of the MOP, paid his second visit to Kingston, having previously spent a month with the Brothers five years earlier. As with all visitors to the MOP centers he was both moved and shocked by his experience. He recalled his time with a young boy, Nicholas, who had been healthy until an injection administered when he was eight-years-old caused him to become totally paralyzed. Handed over to the Brothers when his mother could no longer cope with his condition, Nicholas lay back in his cot all day long with his mouth wide open. Flies had laid eggs in his mouth, which hatched into maggots. Father Payne found it difficult to cope with the horrific scenario as he was asked to hold the boy's head while one of the brothers meticulously removed the maggots, one by one, with tweezers from the hole that they had burrowed behind Nicholas' front teeth.

Father Payne also experienced the sense of community that the Brothers had fostered amongst the people for whom they cared. He noticed how Sheldon, a man who was incontinent and unable to walk, had taken responsibility for little Marrio, the little boy with hydrocephalus who had returned to the centers after his period of recuperation in New Jersey. Although he could not walk, Sheldon moved around by a combination of sliding and hopping along on his knees, and took it upon himself to feed Marrio every day and change his diapers. Father Payne doubted whether he could have coped with feeding and changing Marrio and was deeply inspired by the way in which Sheldon, so seriously handicapped himself, had taken on the onerous task.

On his earlier visit, in 1994, Father Payne had been sitting on the steps of the chapel at Faith Centre, when he heard "a tremendous volley of gunshots, which sounded as if it was against the iron gate just by me."[2] As the gate was opened, the priest saw crowds of people milling around a man who had been shot in the chest. "Just a few yards away there was a group of young men with strange little conical things on top of their heads, which looked to me as if they were some sort of gang." An ambulance arrived to take the victim to the hospital and it was later reported that he had died of his wounds. He had been involved with the thriving drugs trade in the area and was a victim of the turf war between rival gangs.

Drugs, and the violence associated with them, were a part of life in the ghetto. One of the residents with whom Father Payne worked at the centers was Donavan, a young man who had been involved with drugs in the Jamaican community in London and Miami. He had been shot in Miami and had been paralyzed by the wound. His mother, who lived in one small room in the slums, could not cope with the physical demands

---

2. Father Kenneth Payne, op. cit., p. 73.

of caring for her son, which is why he was living in Faith Centre. Donavan's mother poured her heart out to Father Payne during one of her regular visits, telling him of her devastation at her son's condition. He was her only child.

Although Father Payne's earlier visit to the Kingston ghetto was a baptism of fire, it was nothing compared to the violence that erupted on the streets of Jamaica during his visit in 1999. In April, there had been a huge rise of thirty-five per cent in the price of gas. This would hit the poor the hardest, causing increases in bus fares and the price of food. A two-day strike was called in protest against the price increases and tensions were running high. Father Payne set the volatile scene by invoking the atmosphere of the ghetto in which the MOP centers were located:

> All around Prince of Peace is a red-light district and most of the people were on cocaine. Only a month previously a house just the other side of the wall from the Brothers' enclosure had gone up in flames and this was a brothel. Moreover, there was a ruined building immediately next door and at night it was a frequent hideout for dealers in drugs as well as prostitutes. We were thus in a prime location for violence to break out as a result of the rise in the price of gas. And this, in fact, happened.
>
> In the morning after the announcement, roadblocks were put up and each roadblock seemed to have been set fire to so that the whole city was punctuated with clouds of smoke and flames in the middle of the roads. No traffic was possible.[3]

---

3. Ibid., pp. 77–78.

In the midst of this mayhem, Father Ho Lung arrived at Kingston's airport, returning from one of his regular overseas speaking trips. Brother Ambrose and another Brother set out to pick him up but returned half an hour later. It was impossible to drive anywhere on the ghetto's burning streets and, indeed, it had proved difficult to even get back to Prince of Peace. Hearing of the Brothers' unsuccessful attempt to reach him, Father Ho Lung exhibited his customary fearlessness by finding other means to return to Prince of Peace, risking the dangers en route, by hitching a ride most of the way and walking the rest. With similar fearlessness, the Brothers, unable to use their trucks, walked through the burning streets to the centers, refusing to allow the rising tide of violence to keep them from their service to the poor. Within half an hour of Father Ho Lung's return, as Father Payne remembered, "the gunfire increased alarmingly and suddenly there was a gun battle going on right outside our building. . . . I saw policemen in bullet-proof jackets running hither and thither and firing. A helicopter had been showering tear gas around and it was total bedlam."[4]

The unsuspecting English priest had found himself in the middle of an upsurge in violence that shocked even the hardiest Jamaican veterans of the gun-ridden ghetto:

> Everybody I spoke to later said that they had never known anything like it at all, even in Jamaica. There had been shootings and problems at election times but nothing as bad as this. The whole island including Montego Bay where the trouble was also bad, had ground to a halt as the roads were blocked. I found it strange hearing the gunfire only yards away and looking at the bright colours of the flowers and

---

4.   Ibid., p. 78.

trees around Corpus Christi, the bougainvillaea and
the deep green palms with fruit hanging from them.
So many beautiful things on the island with the sun
shining and the wonderfully warm climate; and yet
man is determined to spoil it all.[5]

Father Payne's pondering of the contrast between the beau-
ties of nature with which the Brothers had surrounded themselves and the ugliness of the violence on the streets beyond
their walls serves as a fitting and sublime metaphor of the presence of the Brothers themselves in the midst of the ghetto. They
shone forth the beauty of Christ's Presence in the midst of man's
malice and were candles in the darkness of man's despair.

The riots lasted three days, during which nine people were
killed, fourteen police officers were injured, six police stations
were attacked, 152 people were arrested, scores of stores were
looted, and dozens of buildings were set on fire.

Undaunted by the simmering threat of violence, Father Ho
Lung visited the slums in the area, accompanied by Father
Payne and Brother Henry. Sympathizing with the plight and
anger of the poor in the wake of the government-imposed rise
in gas prices, he told the men in the ghetto that peaceful protest
was legitimate but that there should be no guns, no fires, and
no looting. "Roadblocks, yes," he told them, "but no shooting."
Within a few minutes a large crowd had gathered around him,
listening intently to his words and signifying their approval.
Father Payne confessed to being "a little apprehensive as it was
just in this area that there had been the gun battle the previous
day." His own anxiety merely served to heighten his admiration

5.   Ibid., pp. 78-79.

for Father Ho Lung who was "fearless" in the midst of this tense and potentially violent situation.[6]

Determined to do something practical to help, Father Ho Lung organized a peaceful protest rally at which Christian leaders from various denominations spoke out against the injustice of the increase in gas prices. The Christian Unity for Peace and Justice rally, as it became known, called for an end to the violence but also for an end to the government-imposed rise in prices. "Ghetto priest rallies Jamaican poor," declared the headline of a local newspaper on April 24. "They call him the Ghetto Priest," the report began, "something of a male version of Mother Teresa, most often seen tramping Kingston's slums in white robe, blue sash and sandals. The fact that he has written a number one reggae single and dozens of musicals, and writes a newspaper column, gives him considerably more street cred than your average clergyman. Now, Father Richard Ho Lung, a soft-spoken, white haired 59-year-old Jamaican, is at the forefront of protests against sweeping tax and price rises." Describing the rally as "an unprecedented protest meeting of Jamaican church leaders," the reporter quoted Father Ho Lung's "fiery attack on the government's tax and price increases and what he said was the abandonment of the poor in Jamaica and elsewhere in the Caribbean":

> "There must be a full rollback of the price rises. I am talking right now," Father Ho Lung told several hundred people from various religious denominations in Kingston's Liguanea Park. "Now! Now! Now!" the crowd chanted as he held his microphone out towards them, pop-singer style.[7]

---

6. Ibid., p. 79.
7. Unidentified press cutting, April 24, 1999.

Once again, Father Ho Lung's direct involvement on behalf of the poor brought instant results. The Prime Minister, P. J. Patterson, phoned Father Ho Lung a few hours after the rally had ended explaining to him that he could not personally annul the tax rises but that he had appointed a crisis committee to review the price increases, which would report on its findings within twenty-four hours, after which the government would act immediately. A few days later, prices were decreased.

The government's arrogance and crass disregard for the needs of the poor had brought blood and burning to the slums of Jamaica. Father Ho Lung's response, and that of the alliance of Christians who had joined him, had humbled the pride of the politicians and, in so doing, had helped to bring a degree of justice and peace to the charred and blood-stained streets. The ghetto priest had once more shown himself to be the bane of the politicians and a boon to the poor.

Chapter Seventeen

....

THE GHETTO PRIEST
AT SIXTY

IN THE wake of the riots, a journalist visited the MOP centers and commented that they were located "in areas of
Kingston where this week's violence was worst, where roads
are still blocked and where local gang leaders still rule." Clearly
nervous, the journalist seemed comforted by the prayers of the
Brother assigned to escort him to the centers: "If there was ever
any doubt about the continuing danger, Brother Savio, a young
Indian volunteer, recited a prayer in his car before we drove
into the slums."[1] The Brothers, however, always pray when setting off for the centers, regardless of the perceived level of danger. As such, and unbeknownst to the unsuspecting reporter,
Brother Savio's prayer was an expression of his everyday faith
not an expression of fear of this particular day's danger.

On the day after the visit to the centers by this local journalist, two English reporters from the BBC were shown round
the centers by Father Payne who, as an English visitor himself,
seemed the natural choice to be their guide. "They met Marrio,
the hydrocephalus child, and Jack, whose scalp had been eaten
by maggots, and Rasheen, the three-year-old child with AIDS,

---

1. Unidentified press cutting, April 24, 1999.

183

whose mother's dying wish—she also had AIDS—was that the Brothers should look after her child." Not surprisingly, Father Payne reported that his compatriots were "utterly staggered by all that they saw."[2]

As the streets of Kingston returned to normal after the temporary anarchy of the riots, many soon forgot that normality for Jamaica's poor meant daily misery. In August 1999, four months after the riots, the *Weekend Star* focused on a normal day in the life of the Missionaries of the Poor:

> A homeless man taking what seemed like his final breaths, barely made it to Brothers of the Poor on North Street on Wednesday evening. "Mi come here because mi think you can help mi," he said, laboring to get the words out.
>
> Almost every day Father Ho Lung and his staff get similar cases. The man in this case, Leroy Young, 51, stumbled into the home suffering from dehydration caused from two weeks of diarrhea. With his skin clinging to his bones and eyes sunken, the man told a sorry tale of his living on the street for the past ten years without anyone to really care for him.[3]

As Brother Rolando gave the homeless man a drink of lemonade, Father Ho Lung phoned around the other centers to see if there was room for one more resident. This scenario was a regular occurrence, Father Ho Lung explained. "Every day people that are beaten up or have financial problems come in off the street. Some of them are in such bad condition that two days later they die and we have to bury them. Just last night we

2. Father Kenneth Payne, op. cit., pp. 80–81.
3. *Weekend Star*, August 27, 1999.

were talking about probably having to build another home. All our homes are full. We have people even sleeping in between beds on mattresses."

On September 17, 1999, Father Ho Lung celebrated his sixtieth birthday. To commemorate the occasion the *Gleaner* invited one of the MOP Brothers, Father Ambrose, to write about the legacy that the MOP's Father Founder had bequeathed through his work: "The reggae priest, the renegade priest, the dancing priest, the fiery priest—he has endured all these names that were given to him," Father Ambrose wrote, adding that only one of the many names ascribed to him was really fitting, that of "ghetto priest," the only title that he cherished.

> The ghetto priest—he seeks no human glory. . . . He seeks no earthly riches—the man who heads an international institute that cares for over four hundred homeless and feeds many more in Jamaica, and several hundred overseas, he receives no pay, sleeps in a common dormitory and has only three pairs of his simple religious clothing, wears no watch, keeps no personal bank account or insurance policy, and carries not a cent in his pocket. He seeks no human approval . . . what he seeks is God's approval of his actions and the good of the people. . . .
>
> Father Ho Lung is grateful to the destitute, the homeless, the poor, the unwanted for revealing to him the hidden treasure of the Gospel (the Beatitudes). He is grateful to the Catholic Church and the many benefactors who support his works with the poor. Then there are those men who left the security of their countries, families, jobs and careers behind to join him in working with the poor. "But," Father Ho Lung says, "above all it is to God we owe

the deepest gratitude, the one for whom nothing is impossible."

Yes, he is the ghetto priest, the father of the poor and the rejected. But it is his deeply passionate love for God that makes him love his fellow beings so radically. It is his desire to be at His service that puts him at the feet of the poor. When a friend asked him what he would like for his sixtieth birthday, his answer (as you can expect) was, "I want help to refurbish a building to make a home and training centre for street children."

God bless you, Father Ho Lung, and we wish you a happy sixtieth birthday! May you have many more fruitful years of service in His vineyard.[4]

Another delightful and insightful tribute to Father Ho Lung on the occasion of his sixtieth birthday was provided by P. J. Stewart, a lay associate of the Missionaries of the Poor and a well-known artist in Jamaica. As she explained with evident enthusiasm, the ghetto priest was also, above all, the happy priest:

Happy? No wealth, no wife, no riches, and happy? Working with the poor in the ghettoes of Kingston, day after day, in season and out of season, and happy? No salary, no stipend, no bank account, no insurance policy, and happy? Yes, and he says he is happy, very happy indeed.

What is the secret of his happiness? The Cross, he says. The Cross of Christ! When you can understand the Cross and embrace it willingly, you are the happiest person on earth, he says. And how does he embrace the Cross of Christ? By living a life

---

4. *The Gleaner*, September 18, 1999.

of prayer—each day he spends a minimum of four hours in prayer; by living a life in community with other religious priests and brothers dedicated, like himself, to the service of the poor; by taking care of the poor and the suffering, the homeless and the unwanted, the sick children and those with AIDS. This is the secret of his happiness, he confides.[5]

Steve Gayle, another lay associate, congratulated Father Ho Lung on turning sixty but focused on those Brothers who made his work possible. They, like their Founder, had found true happiness in their poverty and in their service to the poor. "They get no pay. They have no bank account. They have only three sets of clothes but look on their face and you will see a big smile. They are indeed happy. Take a visit to any of their inner-city homes and I guarantee you will be touched. The pain, the suffering, the sickness of the people who live there but more importantly their joy, their happiness and their love will shock you. This is life! This is redemption. This is the Cross of Christ, embrace it and you will discover true happiness."[6]

It would be very easy to scoff at these infectiously enthusiastic accounts of the happiness of Father Ho Lung and the Brothers, and especially perhaps at the claims that the destitute and disabled to whom the Brothers minister are joyful, loving and happy. Surely their lives must be miserable. What do the severely disabled, those dying of AIDS and the homeless have to celebrate? Indeed, if we are tempted to think in unison with the spokesmen of the culture of death, might we not reasonably believe that these people would be better off dead? Shouldn't the disabled have been killed in the womb, sparing them a

---

5.   Unidentified press cutting, September 17, 1999.
6.   *The Gleaner*, September 23, 1999.

"quality of life" that is not worth living? Wouldn't the parents of the disabled have been more responsible if they had snuffed out the defective lives of their children, thereby sparing themselves and the wider community (if such a heartless society can be called a community) the burden of caring for them; and wouldn't they also have been saving the children themselves from the burden of life in such deformed or deficient bodies? And as for seriously ill or disabled adults, or those dying of diseases such as AIDS, wouldn't it be much more humane to offer them euthanasia, the "happy death" that will enable them to escape from their misery and suffering? Such are the questions prompted by a culture which believes that the Cross of suffering must be avoided at all costs. There is in such a culture no "right to choose" for babies who are slaughtered during pregnancy. There is no "right to choose" for the mentally handicapped who are euthanized because they are not able to express their desire to live. It is for this reason that the disabled and destitute at the MOP centers are witnesses for the culture of life and are an affront to the culture of death. Anyone who visits the centers, and this should serve as a challenge to the scoffers and the denizens of the death-culture, will see the joy and happiness on the faces of those who live there. They will experience the love that the residents have for those who visit them, the love that they have for the Brothers who serve them, and the love that they have for each other. Theirs is a life that is not merely endured but enjoyed to the full.

If all men are created equal, it has nothing to do with the wealth or the abilities with which they are lucky or unlucky enough to inherit at birth. In this sense, we are clearly not "equal" but are radically different. If all men are created equal, it is because they are created in the image of God. It is for this reason that Father Ho Lung and the Brothers see the face of

Christ in the faces of the poor and disabled. Only those who reject this divine presence in man can see in the faces of the poor and disabled the features of a sub-human and disposable "reject" or "loser." Only those who reject the divine presence in man can deny others the right to choose life while simultaneously giving themselves the right to kill others on the altar of convenience. The disabled and homeless in the MOP centers serve, therefore, as powerful witnesses of the desire for life and the power of love. In this they were at one with the ghetto priest who had built the centers in which they had found the life and love that is the secret of joy and happiness. Seeing such joy on the suffering face of Christ in his brothers and sisters was the greatest birthday present that the ghetto priest could desire. He was indeed a very happy man.

Chapter Eighteen

....

HEDONISM AND THE
HEART OF DARKNESS

ALTHOUGH Father Ho Lung did not seek human glory or earthly riches, the world continued to bestow its awards and honors upon him. He was inducted into the Caribbean Hall of Fame on the day after his sixtieth birthday for his "humanitarian work," to which he responded by reminding those who were thus honoring him that he was not primarily a philanthropist: "I am not a social worker or purely humanitarian. I am a simple servant of God."[1] Another honor bestowed upon him as he celebrated his sixtieth birthday was the announcement by one of Jamaica's most respected and successful dance companies that it would be honoring Father Ho Lung for the duration of its 1999 season of dance. The priest had been chosen, the dance company's founder explained, "because of the awe-inspiring work he has been doing in the arts to elevate a great number of the dispossessed masses, who had fallen victim to poverty and depression."[2]

At Christmas, Father Ho Lung praised the Jamaican automotive supplies company, Caribrake, for its longstanding

---

1. *The Gleaner*, September 18, 1999.
2. *The Star*, August 7, 1999.

commitment to the work of the Missionaries of the Poor. Every Christmas for the previous twelve years Caribrake had "brought joy to our homeless and destitute" by supplying a fully festive Christmas meal and a gift for all the residents of the centers and also for those on the weekly food lines. This commitment to the poor had grown every year as the work of the MOP had expanded throughout the ghetto. The number of meals and gifts one year was five hundred; it was seven hundred the next, then nine hundred, and by 1999 was more than a thousand. The staff of Caribrake arrived in person to hand out the gifts and serve the food. "They share our the food, feed our retarded, our elderly, the blind and crippled, the deaf and the mute," said Father Ho Lung. "The forgotten ones are remembered and treated with respect by these friends of ours."[3] Quoting Psalm 41 (*Blessed is he who considereth the poor: the Lord will deliver him in time of trouble*), Father Ho Lung was clearly grateful for the Christmas spirit and corporate *caritas* that Caribrake had continued to bestow on the poor of the centers over the years:

> Our "food line" people from the streets also come to the Faith Centre and have a hearty meal with Christmas songs on their lips. Between mouthfuls there were prayers, singing and even dancing. As the Caribrake staff feed our people and give out gifts as well as sing and pray with our poor there is nothing but service, sacrifice and a deep sense of satisfaction on their faces. They have really become a part of our family over the years.

Apart from the beneficence at Christmas, Caribrake also put new tires on each of the MOP vehicles annually and helped with other aspects of the Brothers' ministry. Father Ho Lung wished

---

3. *Weekend Observer*, September 17, 1999.

the company success and prosperity because their "bread was always broken and shared with the least of their brothers and sisters."

In February 2000, Father Ho Lung and Friends released a new album, *I Will Serve You*, which was designed to be an appetizer for the new musical extravaganza, *Jesus 2000*, the largest and most ambitious musical production that they had ever staged. Whereas their previous annual musical productions had been staged at Kingston's Little Theatre, which seated six hundred and thirty people, the new show would be staged at Jamaica's national arena, which seated six thousand people. The size of the cast of singers and dancers was also much larger than anything attempted in previous years, and the music would be provided by a philharmonic orchestra from Florida. Father Ho Lung proclaimed that *Jesus 2000* would be the "greatest and best" production that he and his "Friends" had ever produced. "I want it to be grand, bold and risky but to honour Him. I want to see our people really renewed in Christ, because when people are renewed in Christ, nothing is impossible."[4]

For neither the first nor last time, Father Ho Lung had been led by faith to take on something more challenging than ever. There was no stage at the national arena, no chairs, no sound, no lights. The stage and set had to be built by hand by the Brothers and by volunteers; the chairs, lighting, and sound had to be found from somewhere. There was absolutely no budget so everyone had to volunteer their labor without charge, and everything necessary to make the show a success had to be supplied gratis by benefactors. "It's such a community exercise," Father Ho Lung explained in 2011, looking back over the annual events at the national arena, of which *Jesus 2000* was the

---

4. Unidentified newspaper cutting , February 5, 2000.

first. "There are the singers and the Brothers and the host of lay volunteers. The whole community is involved. All the costumes are billed, free of charge. Everything is billed free of charge." With a truly contagious charm and charisma, Father Ho Lung had succeeded in persuading the wider Jamaican community to emulate the example of the Brothers by offering themselves in free service to the poor.

Jesus 2000 opened on March 31 and was a huge success, setting the high standard that Father Ho Lung would continue to achieve every year thereafter. After its successful run at the national arena, the show went on the road to other Caribbean islands, and also to Florida and New Jersey. The proceeds from ticket sales went toward Ho Lung's plans to build a new home for handicapped children in the Kingston ghetto, which opened in September 2001. Bethlehem Home, as it is now called, is home to sixty severely handicapped babies and children. Apart from the money raised from the shows, donations continued to come in from corporate entities and also from foreign governments. In February 2000, the Japanese government donated $82,780 to the Missionaries of the Poor, Father Ho Lung being invited to the Japanese Embassy to receive the gift from the ambassador.[5] In the same month, senior executives from the oil company, Shell, donated $100,000.

On April 8, Father Ho Lung gave the keynote address to nine hundred Catholics at a convocation in the Bronx at which Father Benedict Groeschel, in many ways the American counterpart to the Ghetto Priest, was also present. In his address, Father Ho Lung warned of the dangers of "pseudo-Christianity" in which even practicing Christians could fall into the trap of placing money, sex, and the desire for worldly power above the true

---

5. *The Gleaner*, February 18, 2000.

God. Such false gods must be laid aside, he said. "All Christians are called to holiness," he added, connecting the self-sacrificial life of the Christian with an embrace of the Cross. "Until you have confronted the Cross, you are not a Christian."[6]

On July 30, Father Ho Lung found himself once again at the center of a political storm of his own making. In a public outburst reminiscent of his earlier tirades against the injustice surrounding Eventide Home and the Gun Courts, he wrote an open letter to a millionaire hotelier CEO in which he condemned the overtly hedonistic character of two hotels, provocatively named Hedonism II and Hedonism III, which the CEO owned. "Being a matter of national importance," Father Ho Lung began, "I now write as a priest—begging, praying, even demanding—that you, John, change the hotels' names and that the activities now being pursued also be changed." The Ghetto Priest's fury was palpable as the open letter continued:

> I received a few telephone calls from friends in Pittsburgh and Baltimore in the US. They were shocked at the advertisement and the portrayal of Jamaica—as a playground for any type of sexual pleasure. And this was seen on Cable TV including the Playboy Channel.
>
> Hedonism, by definition, is a vision of life that pleasure is our final end. Carnal pleasure of all types, sexual excesses, gluttony, drinking, carousing are the features of hedonism.
>
> At Hedonism III there is the promise of the ultimate in carnal pleasure. I don't know how much further Hedonism can be taken. But as it is now, I understand from patrons that have been at Hedonism II that they were so disturbed that they

6. *Catholic New York*, April 13, 2000.

had to leave. Now Hedonism III promises to be even more vulgar. . . .

The patrons are saying that nudity occurs just about anywhere on the beaches and in other parts of the hotels. I was also told that the discotheques, particularly at Hedonism III, allow for nude dancing. . . .

Yes, revenue is coming into Jamaica but at what price, John?

Making Jamaican hotels as a snake pit for those who seek to be hedonists and promoting your hotels as hedonistic is contrary to the Gospel message. It is the promotion of sin and baseness at the lowest level of bestiality. . . .

I do ask you to take into consideration the words of the Lord: "You cannot serve God and Mammon." I pray for you, your family, and the hotel industry. . . . The end—economic prosperity— must be justified by moral means. . . .

I wish you well in business but once dealing with business, we must all be reminded of Christ's question: "What does it matter if you gain the whole world and suffer the loss of your own soul?"[7]

Father Ho Lung's words fell on deaf ears and Christ's question remained unheeded. The CEO responded with anger at the priest's attack upon him but remained defiantly unrepentant. A few months later he outraged many and incurred further criticism from Father Ho Lung when he staged a mass nude wedding at one of his hotels. No doubt, like the aging and morally shriveled Hugh Hefner, he will have his reward.

A month after scolding the CEO, Father Ho Lung launched

7. *Sunday Observer*, July 30, 2000.

a broadside against Jamaica's politicians, blaming them for the continuing violence on the streets that had left thousands dead, and calling on the Prime Minister, the security minister and the police commissioner to resign.

On July 28, Father Ho Lung visited the MOP mission in Haiti. The purpose of the visit was to bless the newly built chapel but also to survey other recent developments in the mission, including the building of a new road, the renovation and repainting of the MOP center, which was home to 150 destitute people, and the installation of a well for fresh water supply and a solar power unit for lighting. He was shocked by the degree of poverty he witnessed, which was even worse than that in the ghettoes of Kingston.

> We walked about in the slums, and I felt a great overwhelming pity for the dreadful sufferings of the people. Babies, hundreds of them were malnourished. . . . My heart ached. . . . Sewage filled the gullies built along the sides of the main streets. There was mess, urine, garbage, flies, pigs. . . . My heart was broken. We had to cover our noses as we walked in the streets, there was so much dust and many of our Brothers had gotten stomach viruses. Others had gotten malaria because of the terrible sewer problems.

Father Ho Lung returned to the MOP center for the destitute with a determination to build a new residence for starving children. "I could not eat or sleep at night, so I prayed. I prayed for Haiti, the poor, our Brothers, for God's guidance and strength. I thanked God for the gift of life, but my heart was so heavy and full of agony."[8]

_____

8. Unidentified press cutting, August 11, 2000.

Although it felt like there was a mountain to climb in order to serve the ongoing needs of the poor, Father Ho Lung was consoled by the knowledge that the Missionaries of the Poor were making a real contribution. By the summer of 2000 there were 115 Brothers serving in the centers in Jamaica, Haiti, India, and the Philippines. In Haiti, the MOP helped to feed 20,000 hungry people, as well as providing a residence for 150 of the country's most destitute people. In the Philippines they provided free schooling to the children of the slums, as well as providing a home for many street children and the mentally handicapped. In India, the Brothers cared for lepers, as well as for abandoned and destitute children. In September, the MOP opened their first mission in Africa. The center in Uganda would care for those dying of AIDS. The opening of the Ugandan mission heralded a third wave of new vocations, following the first wave from India and the second wave from the Philippines. Today, the ethnic composition of the Missionaries of the Poor is defined by the aggregate of these three successive waves. About 40 percent of the Brothers are from the Philippines with the remainder consisting mostly of men from India, Kenya, and Uganda.

Perhaps, in microcosm, the development of the Missionaries of the Poor is a prophetic vision of the shape of things to come in the worldwide Church. As the West disintegrates into deconstructed particles, devoid of faith or reason and lusting after the nihilism of the culture of death, it will take the healthy and vigorous Christians of the so-called Third World to re-evangelize Christendom, bringing the light of faith, hope, and love to the faithless, hopeless and loveless barbarians of the "post-Christian" wasteland. The Missionaries of the Poor are powerful witnesses to the purgatorial power of suffering in the midst of the hell of hedonism and its heart of darkness.

Chapter Nineteen

SUFFER THE LITTLE CHILDREN

Suffer the little children and forbid them not to
come to me; for the kingdom of heaven is for such.
—Matthew 19:14

ANYONE who visits Bethlehem for the first time will be changed forever by the experience. The Bethlehem to which I refer is not the town in Palestine but the center for seriously handicapped children in the ghetto of Kingston, Jamaica, run by the Missionaries of the Poor and opened in September 2001. My own first experience was almost ten years later, in March 2011, and I can honestly say that I will never be the same again. I approached with considerable trepidation, doubting my ability to cope with the horror and squalor that I expected to see. Perhaps, I thought, or at least forlornly hoped, it would not be quite as horrible and alarming as I feared. It was, in fact, worse. Upon arrival the stench of urine assaulted the nostrils and hammered its way into the senses. Seconds later the eyes met the twisted and tangled bodies of broken childhood. There, in rows of cribs, one after another, children of all ages, from babies to teenagers, wriggled and squirmed in various degrees of helplessness. To my uninitiated gaze, it looked almost infernal, a place where the triumph of suffering seemed to call for the abandonment of all hope. It was March 26, the day after the historical date of the Crucifixion,[1] the most hopeless date in the whole of history; the date on which Christ laid dead in the tomb and on which Creation itself screamed in the agonized silence of the vacuum created by His Real Absence. As I looked in stunned silence at the unwanted and abandoned dregs of humanity, bent by the brokenness of body or brain, it seemed to my own broken body and brain that God was indeed dead and buried. If He existed, He seemed to have deserted His creatures in the desert of their woes.

And then it happened. Forcing myself beyond the momentary paralysis with which I'd been struck, I approached a girl of around eight-years-old lying supine in her crib. As I took her hand, she returned my forced smile with a radiance of her own that transfigured the situation and exorcised the demons from my hardened heart. It was a moment of revelation. I was now seeing with the eyes of the young missionary brothers. Looking up at me was the radiant face of the child Jesus. (In as much as ye have done it to the least of these my brothers, ye have done it to me.)[2] I had managed the barest of frozen-hearted and forced smiles in an act of sullen and stubborn duty. She had returned my pathetic effort with a smile that beamed with the light and delight of heaven itself. I had given so little; she had given so much. I finally understood. I understood as Father Ho Lung understood. It was then that I recalled some words of wisdom given to me a few days earlier during a discussion about children with Down Syndrome. "Most of us are sent to

---

1. The Church Fathers and the Mediaeval Church believed that Christ was crucified on March 25. It is likely that this belief has its origin in the memory of the Crucifixion itself, as recounted by the Mother of Christ and St. John, who were present as the event unfolded.
2. Matthew 25:40.

learn," the sage had told me, "but some of us are sent to teach." This little girl had just taught me a priceless lesson that I shall never forget.

This one small incarnational moment was nothing less than a reflection of the Incarnation itself. God had made Himself as helpless in the womb of a young girl in Nazareth as He had made Himself helpless in the broken body of this smiling young girl in the Jamaican ghetto. And, lest we forget, March 25 is the date of the Annunciation as well as the date of the Crucifixion. The Jesus who was laid in the tomb on March 25 was conceived in the womb on the same date. My first infernal impressions could not have been further from the reality before me. I was not visiting a hell without hope, but was receiving a vision of heaven. I was seeing Paradise through the eyes of a child. And in the eyes of that child, the child in me was being born. Such was the miracle of birth that I received in this other Bethlehem.

It should be added that my own experience has been echoed by countless others who have come to Bethlehem since the center was opened more than a decade ago. One experience of Christmas at Bethlehem, recalled by Jeanne Croskery, a long-time lay associate of Brother Ho Lung and the Missionaries of the Poor, is particularly powerful:

> One year, I invited everyone I know in Jamaica to come to Bethlehem for a few hours on Christmas Day to share themselves with those who had no-one. I was surprized at the ones who came . . . mostly non-Catholics! One, my cousin, Maxine . . . a very "stush," uptown lady, who is anti-Churches/ religion. . . . You could've knocked me down when I saw her in the doorway, so I hurried over to thank her for coming, and saw the stunned look on her face. I said, shall I take you around & introduce

you to some of the kids? She said no. She felt overwhelmed & didn't know what to expect, so what
should she do? I said whatever you feel comfortable
doing. She looked at me like I was insane, & said
she'd just sit in a chair at the door & watch for a
while. So I said great. A while later when I looked
over, she had Peter (who could walk) on her lap! I
went & asked her if she was OK, & she said yes, this
little boy just came & climbed on her lap, & was that
OK? I said fine, if you're OK with that.

When Maxine tried to get up to move her car,
which was blocking another vehicle, Peter wouldn't
let her go. She said what do I do? I said oh take him
with you. She was back a few minutes later, & her
face was transformed. I asked her what happened?
She told me that this child was so excited & joyful to
be sitting in her car! I laughed & told Maxine the he'd
probably never been in a car before . . . maybe not
even an MOP truck! She said his face was just alight
when the radio came on & the airconditioning! She
said she has never seen a child look so thrilled. She
was deeply affected by the fact that something she
takes for granted & doesn't even think about could
be a source of such wonder for a child.

That was 4 years ago, & Maxine *still* talks about
that experience to me & others. She asks about
Peter & says she will never get over that feeling of
something so simple bringing such joy, & how it
made her think. . . .[3]

Jeanne's story and the experience of Maxine are typical.
Bethlehem is a place where broken children love and are loved
but also a place where broken visitors are healed. It is a place

3. Jeanne Croskery, correspondence with the author.

where hardened hearts are broken that they may learn to love more fully. As Oscar Wilde discovered through his own self-inflicted suffering, "God's eternal Laws are kind and break the heart of stone":

> Ah! happy they whose hearts can break
>   And peace of pardon win!
> How else may man make straight his plan
>   And cleanse his soul from Sin?
> How else but through a broken heart
>   May Lord Christ enter in?[4]

Jane Rodgers, one of the many lay associates who have been enriched by contact with the Missionaries of the Poor, has visited the centers many times. She remembers the first time and its life-changing impact:

> On my first trip, I thought the Lord had made a mistake. He must have meant for another Jane Rodgers to be there because I didn't think I could do this work. It was so hard seeing the children and adults, the sounds and the smells. Shamefully, I actually thought about going home. But something kept me there and it was only prayer, through the day and at night, that kept me going. . . . totally relying on the Lord for His strength. For the first time in my life I felt Him lifting me up and allowing me to see the beauty in these people rather than their sadness or deformities. My last day there I cried because I didn't want to go home . . . I had fallen in love. What a joy![5]

---

4. Oscar Wilde, "The Ballad of Reading Gaol" (1898).
5. Questionnaire response, January 2012. Questionnaires were sent to a number of lay associates of the Missionaries of the Poor. I have used these, as appropriate, to illustrate the impact that the Missionaries of

Another visitor recognized instantly that the poorest of the poor, crippled and broken in body, were actually healthier and happier, and therefore paradoxically wealthier, than those in rich cultures, such as the United States, who have everything the world has to offer but remain spiritually penurious: "My initial reaction when I saw the residents of the center was the happiness and love they had. I didn't see their suffering, but realized how much we are suffering because of our selfishness. I saw how everyone helped each other to the best of their ability with the gifts and talents God gave them. I realized that this is true peace and happiness, unlike the self-centered life that is common in the world with which we are familiar."[6] This view was echoed by a lay associate who first visited Bethlehem and the other centers in January 2004. "Although the people are suffering physically, once you get to know them you see that they are not suffering emotionally. The people in the centers have so much to teach us."[7]

The poor have so much to teach us and we, the relatively rich, have so much to learn.

---

the Poor have had on those who visit the centers and also to share their insights.
6.   Questionnaire response, January 2012.
7.   Ibid.

Chapter Twenty
....

BROTHER FRANCIS
AND SISTER DEATH

Be praised, my Lord, through our Sister Bodily Death,
from whose embrace no living person can escape.
Woe to those who die in mortal sin!
Happy those she finds doing your most holy will.
The second death can do no harm to them.

Praise and bless my Lord, and give thanks,
and serve him with great humility.

—St. Francis of Assisi

MILLIONS more people learned of the work of Father Ho Lung and the Missionaries of the Poor towards the end of 2000 when EWTN, the global Catholic television network, aired *The Ghetto Priest*, a thirteen-part series on the MOP and its founder. This was the first of several series Ho Lung filmed for EWTN as the ghetto priest proved popular with EWTN's worldwide audience. The series was the fruit of the friendship that had developed between Father Ho Lung, Father Benedict Groeschel, and EWTN's foundress, Mother Angelica. These three feisty founders of religious orders had much in common, their lives paralleling each other almost uncannily. Their coming together in collaborative union was indeed a triumphant triumvirate, a *ménage* made in Heaven.

Father Groeschel, like Father Ho Lung, had felt called to leave the religious order in which he had taken vows in order to found a new order dedicated to a vibrant and revitalized commitment to the poor. With seven other Franciscan brothers, he founded the Franciscan Friars of the Renewal in 1987 and set out to work with the poor in the ghettoes of New York. Like Father Ho Lung, Father Groeschel was no stranger to controversy, defending the Faith vociferously and speaking out courageously against injustice, and, like Father Ho Lung, his robust and radical commitment to God and neighbor has reaped a fruitful harvest. Today, the Franciscan Friars of the Renewal number about 120 priests and brothers who work with the poor in missions in the United States, England, Ireland, and Central America. It was, therefore, no surprise that the two ghetto priests should learn of each other's work, nor that they should become friends.

In August 1998, at Father Groeschel's instigation, he and Father Ho Lung appeared together as guests on Mother Angelica's live program on EWTN. This was Father Ho Lung's first meeting with Mother Angelica, with whom he formed an instant friendship. He recognized "in the twinkle in her eye and the wiggling of her eyebrows" a kindred spirit who shared his and Father Groeschel's joyfully mischievous sense of humor. Like the two ghetto priests, Mother Angelica was a pioneering spirit. She had founded a religious order, the Franciscan Missionaries of the Eternal Word in 1987, the same year in which the Franciscan Friars of the Renewal were founded, but is best known for her founding of the Eternal Word Television Network on the Feast of the Assumption (August 15), 1981, four weeks after Father Ho Lung had founded the Missionaries of the Poor. Impressed by her first encounter with Father Ho Lung, Mother Angelica sent a camera crew to the Kingston ghettoes to film the work of the MOP. It would be the beginning of the MOP's ongoing collaboration with EWTN, leading to the building of a TV studio on the grounds of Corpus Christi, one of the MOP's two religious houses in Kingston, in 2010.

The Franciscan connection continued in June 2002 when Father Ho Lung was awarded the Poverello Medal by Franciscan University of Steubenville, Ohio. Named in honor of St. Francis of Assisi, "the little poor man (Il Poverello)," the Medal was given to Father Ho Lung "in recognition of great benefactions to humanity exemplifying in our age the Christlike spirit of Charity that filled the life of St. Francis of Assisi." Father Ho Lung once again followed in the illustrious footsteps of Mother Teresa, who had received the Poverello Medal in 1976, twenty-six years earlier, when she was a joint recipient with Dorothy Day, founder of the Catholic Worker movement. Father Groeschel, following in Father Ho Lung's footsteps, would receive the Medal in 2011.

At the end of July, Father Ho Lung and Friends performed before the Pope and more than a million young pilgrims at World Youth Day in Toronto. Father Ho Lung was also one of four leading Catholics to be asked to address the Pope and the pilgrims at Toronto's Downsriver Park. The other three were Father Groeschel, Jean Vanier, the founder of L'Arche, an international network of communities for those with developmental disabilities, and Chiara Lubick, founder of the Focalare Movement. Interviewed on the day before he flew to Canada to take part in the momentous event, Father Ho Lung was clearly delighted at the honor that he and the Missionaries of the Poor had received from the Pope. "It's just tremendous," he said.

"We seem to have caught the imagination of Rome."[1]

Back in Jamaica, Father Ho Lung announced that the Brothers would offer a home to any babies of unwanted pregnancies if it would save them from being aborted by their mothers. In a powerful article, "An Alternative to Abortion," he issued a heart-wrenching lament on behalf of the silent victims of *in utero* infanticide:

> Babies in the womb are the most helpless and dependent of all human beings. They are silent even when being destroyed. I have watched films taken of these little ones in their mothers' wombs. They wriggle away from the sharp object placed in the mother's womb; they resist any suction device placed in the womb of the mother. Theirs is a silent cry; a silent protest against death.[2]

Once again, Father Ho Lung was emerging as the champion of the most weak and helpless in society, in this case giving voice to the silent screams of the unborn, those slaughtered innocents whose cries of pain went unheard and unheeded in the vicious vacuum of the culture of death's vacuous nihilism.

On September 3, the godfather or grandfather of the Missionaries of the Poor, Archbishop Samuel Carter, died. For the final five weeks of his life, as he fought with the pain and debilitation of terminal cancer, the MOP Brothers had been with him every night, comforting him and sleeping on the floor by his bedside until morning. His death brought forth from Father Ho Lung's pen the most poignant of tributes and the most moving of meditations on the mystical reality of death:

---

1. *Daily Observer*, July 25, 2002.
2. *Weekend Observer*, July 12, 2002.

We loved him very much. He was truly the spiritual grandpa of the Missionaries of the Poor. It was
under him that the first permission was given to
form Missionaries of the Poor in 1981. On the part
of his consultors it was not a popular decision, but
Archbishop swept aside all misgivings and objections and decided against the general consensus
that it not be allowed. . . .

For thirty-five nights the Brothers slept on the
floor in Archbishop Carter's bedroom at Holy
Cross Rectory. . . . He would sit up and tell stories
about the Lord, about the saints, and about his
experiences as Archbishop. . . . His eyes were full of
warmth and friendliness. . . . After making sure he
was comfortable . . . the Brothers would fall asleep
on the floor. . . . Archbishop Carter would sleep a
few hours [and then] tiptoe . . . to the bathroom.
He laughed and told me how one night he stepped
on an arm, on another night it was a leg, and then
on another night it was almost a mop-headed MOP.
He jokingly called us the "mops," the clean-up men
who picked up the debris of humanity, once cast off
or forgotten by society.

Following a swift decline, the Archbishop was admitted to
the University Hospital. Father Ho Lung, accompanied by
Father Ambrose, rushed to the hospital to see him.

He greeted me with a great big warm smile, and we
held hands for a long time. I could feel tears welling
up in me. . . . "It's near the end, I can tell," he said.
He kissed my hands. I hugged him. . . . We prayed
over him, blessed him, and asked him if he needed
anything. When he was in a seizure of pain he asked

us to turn our faces away; when the pain was gone he welcomed us with a smile once gain.

Thus it was all night long. . . . When he died at 1:15 on Tuesday morning, the Brothers were at his side, holding his hands.

That smile he had on his face has remained deep in my soul. It was so beautiful. . . . All along in his life he was masterly, masculine, direct and decisive. On his deathbed he was gentle and like a child with the most enchanting smile. He never stopped smiling between his immense and agonizing attacks of pain. Why that continuous smile? Archbishop wanted us to celebrate at his death, to laugh, to be happy. He was about to enter heaven's doors, to be with the Father and all the saints and angels. He was giving witness in the most profound way at the most difficult time in any man or woman's life. Just at the point of being engulfed by that cynical and frightening reality of death, when this entire world would come to a closure and most would scream in terror, Archbishop Carter was at his happiest! Gladly and fearlessly he accepted death. What a statement of faith! What a call to live out the depth of our true self—Christ in complete service of others, Christ on the cross about to deliver His human body to the place of skull! But no, it was not Golgotha; rather it was to deliver Himself to God's heavenly kingdom. His smile defied death and will encourage us forever, for those who live in the Lord, work in the Lord and die in the Lord, there is only heaven. . . .

Grandpa, I am sad, the Missionaries of the Poor are sad, all of us Jamaicans and Catholics are sad. But we know you are happy and you want us to be happy. Thus you have forced us to be happy at

your death—correction—at the moment of your
entrance into heaven.[3]

In the same way that the death of the Archbishop had served
as an edifying *memento mori* for Father Ho Lung, inspiring him
to emulate the Archbishop's example in holiness, a health scare
of his own in the months following the Archbishop's death
brought the prospect of his own mortality dangerously close
to home. He had been experiencing chest pains for some time,
which he had sought to alleviate, following his doctor's advice,
by a change of diet, regular exercise and the avoidance of stress-
ful situations. Although the healthier lifestyle seemed to help,
the chest pains persisted. After a close friend suffered a massive
heart attack, he felt prompted to phone Dr. Gerry Bortolazzo,
an Atlanta-based physician and good friend, remembering his
words, "Any time you have a problem just call me."[4] At Dr.
Bortolazzo's insistence, Father Ho Lung flew from New Jersey
where he was performing a concert to Atlanta in November
2003, accompanied by Father Brian Kerr, one of the MOP
founders who had just returned from ten years at the helm
of the MOP's mission in the Philippines. Dr. Bortolazzo met
them at the airport, and told Father Ho Lung that he needed
to take care of himself if he wanted to continue taking care of
others. Bortolazzo was aware that Father Ho Lung had failed
the heart stress test in Jamaica, and so he drove him directly to
the emergency room at nearby Cobb Hospital for an immediate angioplasty.

Father Ho Lung, as poor and penniless as those he served,
found himself in the novel position of being the recipient of

3. *Sunday Gleaner*, September 8, 2002.
4. Father Ho Lung, "Diary of a Ghetto Priest," *The Gleaner*, November 24,
   2003.

the sort of charity for which he normally begged on behalf of others. Like little Marrio who had been flown to the United States five years earlier for the operation to alleviate the effects of hydrocephalus, Father Ho Lung found himself the grateful and indebted beneficiary of the sort of free service to the poor, which he normally practiced himself. His gratitude was evident in his Diary entry a few weeks later. "I am alive! This is a gift from the Lord passed through the hearts, minds and hands of my beloved friends":

> The open heart surgery was scheduled without cost for the very next day. I felt like a child in the hands of God and my friends. I could only trust in God's guidance, which has never failed me. I know that it was obedience to God and the truth that led me to the Cobb Hospital in Atlanta. It was also love and affection on the part of the good Lord and my dear friend Gerry who delivered me into the hands of a wonderful cardiologist, Dr. Bob Warner, and the surgeon, Dr. David Langford, in the most renowned heart surgery hospital in the US, St. Joseph's. Again, free of cost. Father Brian and I offered morning prayer for that day and I received communion. The opening of the Psalm read, "My heart is ready oh God, my heart is ready." God's love, God's guidance and protection, His words and His close presence in times of great danger and difficulty were truly evident to me.
>
> The operation was a miracle. What loving friends God has given me! The surgeon, Dr. Langford, did his job perfectly, humbly, and calmly. . . . Everyone was so good.
>
> After the operation, Father Ambrose and my brother Michael came to visit me. My friends

provided accommodations and my other needs in
Atlanta for my post surgery recovery. The Sisters of
Mercy under Sister Valentina Sheridan, as well as
Dr. Langford and Dr. Warner, provided their loving
care, free of any charge. I thank the Lord for such
wonderful friends! I celebrated Mass today humbly
giving thanks for this miracle that took place. God's
grace was upon me during the entire period and I
found myself so quickly recovering.[5]

The complete success of the operation is evident, ten years
later, in the way in which Father Ho Lung dances on stage with
his "Friends" during their concert appearances, or the way in
which he still enjoys a vigorous game of racquetball with the
much younger Brothers. During one of my visits to Kingston in
2011, I asked Father Ho Lung why his arm was in a sling. "Oh,
I sprained it playing racquetball," he chuckled, adding with a
mischievous smile that perhaps he should learn to slow down. I
could see from the glint in his eye that he had no such intention
and that he would resume the racquetball as soon as his wrist
had healed.

Having seen Archbishop Samuel Carter praise the Lord in his
smiling embrace of Sister Bodily Death, from whom, as Brother
Francis exclaimed, "no living person can escape," and having
seen the shadow of Sister Death in his own close encounter
with mortality on the operating table, Father Ho Lung could
echo the words of the holy St. Francis in the final lines to his
Canticle to the Sun:

> Be praised, my Lord, through our Sister Bodily
> Death,

---

5.   Ibid.

from whose embrace no living person can escape.
Woe to those who die in mortal sin!

Happy those she finds doing your most holy will.
The second death can do no harm to them.

Praise and bless my Lord, and give thanks,
and serve him with great humility.

Chapter Twenty-One

....

THE BLOOD OF
THE MARTYRS

IN 2004, Father Ho Lung and Friends had their greatest success to date with the staging of *Moses*, described by Father Brian as having tested the Brothers and Wynton Williams, the music director, to the very limit. "It was labeled the biggest musical ever in the history of Jamaica, and it caused almost a national rejoicing that Jamaica could have produced something so spectacular, so beautiful, and so powerful in theaters. The press just kept echoing the fact that it was the biggest show ever. It was really an epic production." In the same year, the Missionaries of the Poor received a gift of seventy acres of land in Iron River in the mountains north of Kingston. On the highest point of land, the Brothers built the beautiful retreat center, Mount Tabor Monastery. Small scale farming of pigs, rabbits and chickens is practiced on the property. In 2008 the Beatitudes Home for disabled children was built on the grounds.

In September 2004, Father Ho Lung travelled to Rome with Fathers Hayden, Ambrose, and Savio. While enjoying an ice cream outside a cafe near St. Peter's basilica, Cardinal Ratzinger walked by, presumably on his way back to the Vatican after lunch. "It was around two o'clock in the afternoon," Father Hayden remembered. Ratzinger was alone and walking swiftly, "his hands swinging." "Isn't that Cardinal Ratzinger?" Father Ho Lung asked. Two American nuns with whom the priests were talking at the time confirmed that it was indeed the then-Prefect of the Congregation for the Doctrine of Faith, the second most powerful man in the Church. "By that time he had gone quite a ways," recalled Father Hayden, the cardinal's brisk stride belying his seventy-seven years. "Father said go, go fetch him, stop him. In those days Father had a problem with his foot, so he couldn't walk fast. Brother Ambrose, Brother Savio and I ran after the cardinal and stopped him." The three Brothers asked His Eminence if he could wait for a moment while their superior hobbled slowly towards them. Father Hayden was struck by the cardinal's graciousness and patience. "There are millions of religious in Rome but he stopped and started talking to us. He stayed with us for at least twenty minutes. It showed his utter humility." Little could they know that the humble man with whom they spoke would become Pope following the death of John Paul II only seven months later.

Considering the way that the Missionaries of the Poor embraced the mystery of suffering with such pure and paradoxical joy, I wondered what Father Ho Lung thought of John Paul II's own struggle with the debilitating effects of Parkinson's disease. What did Father Ho Lung think about the significance of the way that the Holy Father dealt with his own prolonged suffering in the last years of his life?

"He certainly made the preciousness of suffering very clear," Father Ho Lung responded, "a preciousness which of course would be considered outdated in our times in which people promote euthanasia. No matter what, he gave witness. I began to understand in a real way that his life exemplified the importance of existence in a Thomistic sense. Existence is in itself enough. It is all. The matter of production is subsidiary to existence and just *being*, in itself, is really what is most important. Creation. Being. And this fits in with Franciscan spirituality. The manner in which he lived and through all his suffering, he just kept going on behalf of mankind. That was love. Love in a very serious way."

I remarked to Father Ho Lung that I saw a parallel between his own mysticism of suffering and John Paul II's embrace of the public and grotesque face of pain. In his newspaper column Father Ho Lung was not afraid to shock his readers. He wanted people to see the grotesque and to be confronted or even affronted by it. Similarly it would have been very easy for John Paul II to hide himself away, especially considering that towards the end he could barely speak and was drooling. The descent from the vibrancy of his early papacy to the incapacity visible in his final years was as shocking as anything in Father Ho Lung's "Diary of a Ghetto Priest." "He revealed himself," Father Ho Lung interjected. "Yes, yes," he whispered. "He revealed himself."

I thought I understood and endeavored to articulate the depth of the mystery of suffering into which we had plunged. I suggested that in the poorness of his ugliness the pope had shone forth the transcendent beauty beyond it. For those that had the eyes to see it, of course. I suggested that John Paul II was an incarnate witness to the sort of spirituality of suffering that resides at the very heart of the Missionaries of the Poor. The pope had embraced the philosophy that he was teaching and preaching, allowing people to see him in his pathetic state, so that, in seeing him, they might embrace the hope to be discovered in the very abyss of pain. "Yes," Father Ho Lung agreed. "Yes. Very, very, very much so."

On October 27, 2005, a few months after the death of John Paul II, the Missionaries of the Poor were plunged into their very own abyss of pain when two of the Brothers were shot dead by an unknown gunman. Brother Marco Laspuna, a twenty-two-year-old Filipino, and Brother Suresh Barwa, a thirty-one-year-old Indian, were killed by a single bullet as they were washing dishes in the community's kitchen in Corpus Christi. They were standing side by side at the time and the bullet passed through both their heads. Brother Suresh was killed instantly and Brother Marco died a few hours later. Father Ho Lung was across the street in Prince of Peace when he received a call from Father Ambrose telling him that something terrible had happened. "I ran over and when I went in I couldn't believe it. The Brothers were holding these two Brothers in their arms and there was blood on the kitchen floor and the whole place was very somber and sad, and sort of prayerful. Suresh was dead and the brothers described to me that when he died, when he was hit by the bullet, he just had a sort of querying look in his eyes as if asking why? Then he closed his eyes and then opened them again and smiled. And then he was dead."

Father Brian rushed Brother Marco to Kingston Public Hospital where he died about four hours later. "It was terrible," Father Ho Lung remembered, "but there was oddly a sort of peace over the house. All the Brothers gathered together in the chapel and we had exposition of the Blessed Sacrament. I told the Brothers to collect the blood because I believe that this blood is sacred blood. It was blood that was mingled with the crucified Christ. So we collected the blood and kept it in a Eucharistic cup for a long time. At the exposition, we placed the blood on the altar for the Lord and the brothers prayed and sang songs."

News of the killing travelled fast and the Brothers were soon besieged by reporters and by government officials. Father Ho Lung confessed that he almost resented the intrusion and wished that the Brothers could have been left alone to grieve their loss. The MOP missions in India and the Philippines were called, informing them of the tragic news, and Father Ambrose phoned the families of the two deceased Brothers. "It became very clear to me that Brother Suresh and Brother Marco were martyrs," said Father Ho Lung, "so I told the Brothers that we must use the death of these men to glorify the Lord." In the light of the Resurrected Christ the death of His servants could not be seen simply as a tragedy. "Let their deaths be raised up to the Lord. Then we prayed and we said whatever happens, we must forgive the murderer, whoever he is."

In the immediate aftermath of the killings, and the confusion that accompanied it, there were suggestions that life in the ghetto had become too dangerous. "There was fear. Should we run away? Should we leave the ghetto? Should we continue the work but live somewhere else? All kinds of thoughts went through our minds but it became clear that the Lord wanted us to be exactly where we were."

On the following morning, after Mass and meditation, the Brothers were asked whether they wanted to go to the centers. The response was unanimous. They would not only go to work at the centers as usual but, as a mark of solidarity with both the poor and with their fallen Brothers, they would walk through the streets of the ghetto instead of being taken in the MOP trucks. "Of course, everybody in the ghetto knew about it by this time," says Father Ho Lung, and the people looked on in respectful silence as the Brothers passed by. The residents of the centers were crying and were asking the Brothers whether they would now leave the ghetto. On being told that the Missionaries of the Poor were planning to continue as before, many of the residents and people of the ghetto were astonished. "It was a source of wonder at the meaning of faith, the meaning of commitment. It was really astounding to people all over Jamaica that the Missionaries who are from different countries were so committed to the Jamaican people."

On November 12, the day of the funeral, the two coffins processed through the streets of the ghetto. "It was so beautiful and powerful," remembered Father Ho Lung. "People were saying the rosary, singing songs, and coming up to touch the habits of the Brothers."

"They were Missionaries of the Poor," reported the *Gleaner* newspaper on the day after the funeral, "[but] they were given a farewell fit for a king." After the service at the packed Holy Trinity Cathedral, at which Members of Parliament, entertainers, and high-ranking members of the security forces were present, the huge procession passed through the streets of downtown Kingston. The coffins were on the back of a small truck and the Missionaries, in their customary white habits, their hands clasped before them, walked beside the slow moving vehicle as it made its way through the same inner-city communities in which the slain Brothers had worked. As the coffins wended their way through residential areas, people left their homes to join the procession, many holding burning candles, or paid their respects in silence as the bodies passed by. Others joined spontaneously in the singing of the popular gospel songs that the Missionaries were singing. It was an immensely moving display of communal unity in support of the Brothers.

Father Ho Lung sees a direct connection between the martyrdom of the Brothers and the exponential growth in the size of the MOP, which followed their deaths. "The community began to really grow in terms of numbers at an incredible rate after that." For the non-believer, the huge growth in the number of vocations in the wake of the killing of Brothers Suresh and Marco could be explained or explained away by attributing it to a mere coincidence. For those with faith, such as Father Ho Lung and his band of Brothers, the intercession of their departed brethren with God in Heaven has bestowed graces on the MOP's apostolate of which the dramatic increase in vocations is the miraculous fruit. As all Catholics know, and as history testifies, the blood of the martyrs is the seed of the Church.

Chapter Twenty-Two

BLOOD MONEY AND THE CULTURE OF DEATH

IN 2006, the Missionaries of the Poor, now in their twenty-fifth year, opened a new center for severely disabled children in Cebu in the Philippines. The previous quarter century had been action-packed and there was no sign that the MOP's founding father was slowing down or beginning to show that his sixty-six years were taking their toll. On the contrary, the ghetto priest seemed as irrepressible and indefatigable as ever in his unstinting service to the poor. In August 2007, when Hurricane Dean struck Kingston, he phoned around friends in the United States to raise the necessary funds to buy materials for the repair of a thousand homes. Over the following weeks the Brothers worked tirelessly repairing the roofs of homes in the ghetto.

In December, the MOP opened a new mission in Orissa in Northern India, an area where Hindu fundamentalists had been attacking and persecuting Christians. Once again, the Missionaries of the Poor proved themselves to be fearless front-line soldiers in the evangelizing army of Christ. In August 2008, the anti-Christian persecution in the area forced thousands of Christians to flee to nearby forests. Many priests and religious went into hiding or sought sanctuary as refugees in nearby dioceses. The houses of Christians were burnt, religious statues were broken, Church property was vandalized and churches were burned to the ground. Tabernacles were broken and the Sacred Host profaned. Vehicles and the houses of priests and religious brothers and sisters were damaged or burnt. A Catholic nun was raped and the priest who was with her was severely beaten. Another priest was discovered hiding in a vandalized church and was beaten so badly that he died later of his injuries. Members of the laity were beaten and then buried alive; others were burnt alive or were tortured before being beheaded. Most of the worst of the violence took place to the east of the region in which the MOP mission was established. Though they serve fearlessly in close proximity to this violent area, the Brothers have not been directly affected by the tensions.

In May 2008, the American Friends of Jamaica bestowed its International Humanitarian Award on Father Ho Lung, an award that elicited a congratulatory letter from Jamaica's Prime Minister, Bruce Golding, in which the Prime Minister thanked Father Ho Lung and the MOP for their "tremendous service" to Jamaica.[1] In October the Prime Minster attended a dinner given in Father Ho Lung's honor at the offices of the *Gleaner* newspaper, and later the same year the priest received an official honor from the government itself when he was awarded the Order of Jamaica for his "outstanding contribution to religion and the care of the poor."[2] In October, the MOP established its first mission in the United States, at Monroe, near Charlotte, North Carolina. By the end of the year, the number of Brothers enrolled with the MOP, either as aspirants, postulants, novices,

1.	*The Gleaner*, May 9, 2008.
2.	Unidentified press cutting, August 6, 2008.

or fully professed Brothers, had risen above five hundred for the first time.

In November 2008, Father Ho Lung announced plans to open a new center in Kingston for expectant mothers, a plan that came to fruition three years later with the opening of the Holy Innocents center. As its name implied, the purpose of the new center was to help distressed mothers while at the same time saving their babies from being aborted. "Anyone at all who is pregnant and in a state of panic would be most welcome to come and visit us," said Father Ho Lung. He added that the Brothers would be willing to look after the babies after birth, allowing the mothers to reclaim them at a later date, should they wish.[3]

Two weeks before the announcement of plans for the Holy Innocents center, a newspaper interview with Wynton Williams, music director of Father Ho Lung and Friends, offered a rare insight into the private life of the ghetto priest.[4] Williams had first met Father Ho Lung in the mid-80s, when, as a teenager, he had applied for a singing position with Father Ho Lung and Friends. Wynton's older brother, Jon, was the music director of the "Friends" at the time, a position that Wynton would inherit and which he holds to this day. More than twenty years after their first meeting, Williams stated that "the relationship between Father and me continues to grow and deepen." The newspaper described him as Father Ho Lung's "best friend," an accolade which would seem to be accurate enough with the arguable exception of those Brothers who have worked with the MOP since its founding or from the earliest years, such as Fathers Hayden, Brian, and Ambrose.

---

3. *Sunday Observer*, November 30, 2008.
4. *Sunday Gleaner*, November 16, 2008.

"In the beginning, I wondered how we would relate to each other, based on the age difference," Williams said, "but as the relationship developed, Father became a good friend . . . a pal. At times, he was a father, at other times, a brother, and sometimes a spiritual counselor. On our travels as the performing group, or on his missions overseas where I accompany him to sing or share the Word, it has always been easy to relate to him and to discuss issues. It's amazing how, over the years, we have had differences of opinion but never conflicts. We have a very harmonious relationship." Reading Williams' words, I am reminded of G. K. Chesterton's words about his relationship with his brother, that they were always arguing but they never quarreled. It seems that one of the secrets of life and of love is the ability to argue without quarreling or, in Williams' words, to have differences without conflicts.

Asked what they spoke about when they were alone together, Williams replied that they discussed "life in general, developments in the country and personal issues" and added that Father Ho Lung was very open about sharing his "burdens and challenges." Then, laughing, Williams, who is a Baptist minister, confessed that they also had "theological arguments about faith."

In the interview, Williams offered fascinating revelations about Father Ho Lung's private life, those aspects of his personality so rarely seen by those who know only his public persona. Williams mentioned Father Ho Lung's "special love for nature and plants," and indeed, the beautiful gardens and landscaping of the two MOP religious houses in Kingston represent a veritable oasis in the desert of the ghetto. Apart from the colorful plants, the Brothers also surround themselves with aquaria and aviaries, as well as farm animals. There is, as Father Ho Lung would readily admit, more than a touch of the Franciscan in the former Jesuit. Father's appreciation for the beautiful things of life was evident to me in an anecdote he offered during one of my interviews with him. He told me that some of the Brothers had been concerned that the beautiful surroundings in which they lived lacked the level of asceticism demanded by the religious life. Father Ho Lung responded by asking the Brothers whether brightly colored paint was any more expensive than black paint. In true Franciscan spirit, he is aware that the best and most beautiful things in life are given freely by the Creator of all that is beautiful. It is, therefore, a sin and a singular blindness to not wish to be surrounded by the beautiful things that God provides. Father Ho Lung added a post script to his anecdote, telling me that one of the Brothers who had initially questioned the need for beautiful surroundings had arranged to have the foreign mission to which he was assigned painted in the brightest colors, learning the lesson that there is never a conflict between the ascetic and the aesthetic.

Williams also revealed that Father Ho Lung was something of a sportsman, remarking that he "loves to go fishing when he gets the chance" and is "also quite good at volleyball, which he plays often with the Brothers." Williams also noted that Father Ho Lung "loves cricket." He listed food as Father Ho Lung's "favourite pastime," adding that "he loves, in particular, stew peas and a good steamed fish." And, of course, Williams mentioned the Reggae Priest's love for music. "He's a Jamaican at heart and so his favourite genre is Jamaican mento and folk, but he also has a fine ear for European classical music." Although such insights are interesting, intriguing, and indeed valuable, Williams ended the interview by returning the focus to the really important things in Father Ho Lung's life, those things which, above all others, inspired his love for him as a friend:

Father is a true friend, a confidant and a good support. I love him and could see myself giving my life
for him, because I believe his life is significant to
others because of his service. Father will beg humbly for the poor, even to the point of taking insults,
and yet, he continues to serve and so, because of
whom he is and how he serves others, I would lay
down my life for him.

Father has also had a significant impact on my life
because, while I shared his concern for the country
and the poor, the depth with which Father has challenged my own dedication and commitment to the
cause of Christ. It challenged me to look deeper and
to go deeper in terms of serving the poor.

Father is a wonderful friend and father to me. I
am confident and positive that our friendship was
meant to be, and that by God's grace it will continue.

For all the singular insights that Williams' intimacy with
Father Ho Lung offers to the outsider, such as the priest's love
for nature and sports, it is the universal applicability of these
concluding comments that really matter. In these heartfelt
words about Father Ho Lung's impact on his life, Williams
echoed the views of the Brothers, the lay associates, and the
people of Jamaica who have all been touched by Father Ho Lung
and challenged by his example "to look deeper and to go deeper
in terms of serving the poor." I am reminded also, in Williams'
reference to Ho Lung's willingness to be insulted while begging for the poor, of the example of Mother Teresa, particularly
of the incident in which Mother Teresa approached a wealthy
businessman, her hands held out to him as a beggar. The businessman responded by spitting on her hands. Unperturbed,
the saintly beggar thanked the businessman for offering his

opinion of her, but then repeated her request that he give to the poor. The businessman walked away but the incident tugged at his conscience. He later relented and repented, becoming a generous benefactor to those in need.

As the global financial crisis of the 2000s deepened, the Missionaries of the Poor found themselves even poorer than usual because people give less to charity in times of economic hardship. By the end of 2008 the Brothers had begun chopping wood as fuel for cooking in order to save money on gas. In order to save on the cost of electricity, they had stopped using fans at Corpus Christi and Prince of Peace, the religious houses in which the Brothers lived, though they still used them at the centers at which the poor resided. In order to save on the cost of food they had substituted beans for meat. When they received gifts of meat, they used it more sparingly to make it last longer.

In early February 2009, Father Ho Lung and other Catholic priests refused to make their submissions before the Parliamentary committee responsible for reviewing Jamaica's policy on abortion after only six of the sixteen members of the committee bothered to attend. Of those half dozen who did attend all but one arrived late so that the chairman finally called the meeting to order an hour after its scheduled starting time. Whether the non-attendance and tardiness was the product of indifference to the issue of abortion on the part of the politicians, or was a deliberate snub to the Catholic pro-life position, the priests responded by treating the committee with the indifference it evidently deserved, walking out of the proceedings until such time as their position would be given appropriate time and attention. "This is a major issue of life and death," Father Ho Lung told reporters as he and the other priests walked out of the meeting. The committee's indifference or contempt was "disrespectful," indicating "disrespect for life, disrespect for truth and the issues that are at hand."[5]

Faced with continuing indifference or contempt on the part of the Parliamentary committee, Father Ho Lung and the other priests finally consented to give evidence to the committee three weeks later. Although, once again, only six of the sixteen members of the committee bothered to attend, the priests felt that the pro-life voice needed to be heard to counter attempts to legalize abortion on the island. The occasion found Father Ho Lung at his most forthright and militant, his strident attacks on the disseminators of the culture of death elevating the abortion issue to the national headlines. "Ho Lung says Jamaica must reject 'blood money'" was the headline in the *Sunday Observer*. The "blood money" to which Father Ho Lung referred was the aid that he claimed was being offered to Jamaica by the United States and the European Union on condition that abortion is legalized: "They say, *'if you want our millions and billions of dollars you must agree to legalize abortion. If you want our wealth, men and women must be able to be gay—without that you get no money.'* We must not do what is wrong for the sake of money, no matter how much, no matter how great the temptation. We must do what is right, and God will take care of our nation, our women, our men, and our children."[6]

Singling out the secular fundamentalism of the European Union for particular scorn, Father Ho Lung stated that the EU was being hypocritical in opposing capital punishment whilst supporting abortion. According to such warped logic, murderers and terrorists have a "right to life" but unborn children do not. He also condemned the so-called "pro-choice" movement for being an agent of the descent into moral decay: "Sexual

---

5. *The Gleaner*, February 6, 2009.
6. *Sunday Observer*, March 1, 2009.

liberation is part of the pro-choice movement . . . we will have sex with whomever and whenever we want . . . pro-choice in every area of life has become the foundation of evil in our modern world and Jamaica. The unholy trinity of sex, money, popularity in the name of freedom of choice has brought in the devil himself." Coming from the mouth of a politician, such stridency could be considered a rant, albeit a rant on the side of the angels, but Father Ho Lung managed to convey the facts without seeming to lose his cool or his serenity. According to one reporter, the ghetto priest delivered his broadside against the culture of death, "in a tone almost hypnotic in its calmness and with quiet authority."[7] Although both the EU's envoy to Jamaica and the Director General of the Planning Institute of Jamaica, the body responsible for negotiating aid from the European Union and the United States, denied vehemently that any negotiated loan was subject to the sort of secularist agenda to which Father Ho Lung had referred, only the most naïve of political observers would accept at face value such denials. It is irrefutable that the European Union, and other international financial institutions have sought to link financial aid to the recipients' willingness to conform to the tenets of the culture of death, such as the advocacy of condom use in the absurd belief that promoting promiscuity will promote "women's health." Although Father Ho Lung could offer no documentary evidence in the specific case of Jamaica, the existence of the mechanism of moral subversion in return for aid was not in doubt. Any observer of the smutty world of globalism will know that politicians and aid agencies do most of their dirtiest work behind closed doors and without the grubbiest details ever being documented. Whether the supplier of

---

7. *Sunday Observer*, March 1, 2009.

the "blood money" is the EU, the IMF, the UN, the IRA or Al Qaida, the transaction is seldom easily traceable in terms of a paper trail. The connection between the blood and the money can only be discovered by following the trail of blood back to the money. As such, Father Ho Lung was doing a great service to the people of Jamaica when he alerted them to the pernicious nature of agenda-driven aid.

Chapter Twenty-Three

DEFENDING THE HOLY INNOCENTS

FATHER Ho Lung's uncompromising stance on abortion led to his being criticized vociferously by those who had customarily supported his work. The *Daily Observer*, a newspaper which had always been very supportive of the work of the Missionaries of the Poor, published an editorial under the heading "You're Wrong This Time" in which Father Ho Lung was criticized for describing the "pro-choice" movement as an agent of the descent into moral decay. The newspaper begged to differ:

> Father Ho Lung's view is, we believe, a little extreme. For freedom of choice is one of the pillars of democracy which, over many centuries, has proven to be the best system by which societies are organized and function.
>
> The individual's right to choose does not reside only in governance issues. Rather, it applies in every aspect of the individual's life, and that includes procreation.

> It is our view that decisions on reproduction
> must rest with the individuals directly affected by
> the pregnancy, not the Church or any other anti-
> abortion group or even pro-abortion group.[1]

The naïveté and logical absurdity of the newspaper's "pro-choice" stance beggars belief. It ignores the obvious problem that the exercise of one person's freedom might take away the freedom of another, or that one person's choices inevitably impact the choices of others. What happens if the exercise of my freedom takes away the freedom of another? Should my freedom take precedence over the freedom of the other? What happens if my freedom of choice removes the ability of another to choose freely or perhaps destroys their ability to choose at all? Do I have the freedom to choose to kill another person? If my freedom of choice does extend to such a right, am I not removing the freedom of the person whom I kill? If I do not have the freedom to choose to kill another person, are we not accepting that a limitation on certain freedoms of choice is necessary and desirable? Does a parent have the freedom to choose to kill his or her child? If so, what about the child's freedom? Do children have the same rights to freedom as adults? None of these questions are even addressed in the shallow glibness of the *Daily Observer*'s objection to Father Ho Lung's criticism of the "pro-choice" movement. And yet it must be conceded that the looseness of Father Ho Lung's phraseology left him open to such misunderstanding.

Let's revisit his exact wording to the Parliamentary committee: "Pro-choice in every area of life has become the foundation of evil in our modern world and Jamaica. The unholy trinity of sex, money, popularity in the name of freedom of choice has

---

1. *Daily Observer*, March 9, 2009.

brought in the devil himself." It was Father Ho Lung's apparent condemnation of "choice" itself which led to the *Daily Observer*'s negative reaction to his words. Let's be clear. The Catholic Church holds unequivocally that "freedom of choice" is sacrosanct, in the absolute sense that it affirms that God granted free will to human beings and that this is good. Man was created free and not a mere slave to instinct. The Church also understands, however, that freedom can be abused and that the abuse of freedom invariably makes people less free than they would have been if they had used their freedom properly. The abuse of freedom by one person leads to the removal of freedom from another. This is the economics of freedom, the rules by which freedom is itself governed. It is, therefore, legitimate for laws to be passed to prevent the abuse of freedom by some people if that abuse removes the freedoms of others. In this context, the Church insists that human life is sacred and that human beings should not have the freedom to choose to kill their own children. In this case, the freedom of the child must be protected through the limitations on the freedom of the parent. If Father Ho Lung had phrased his objections to the "pro-choice" movement in these terms, the *Daily Observer* and other "pro-choice" advocates would have had a harder time taking what they perceived to be the moral high ground.

Father Ho Lung understands all this, of course. His view on abortion reflects that of the Church. It is his work for distressed pregnant mothers and for the vulnerable children in their wombs which warrants our praise and not the well-meaning words offered to self-serving politicians. As the agents of the culture of death continued to campaign for the legalization of abortion in Jamaica, Father Ho Lung continued to plan for the opening of Holy Innocents center and began to liaise with pastors of various denominations to present a united front in defence of life. In June he hosted a meeting at Corpus Christi at which around thirty-five pastors attended. A month later, he hosted another breakfast meeting at which one of the leaders of the pro-life movement in Jamaica spoke and in August Father Ho Lung hosted a breakfast meeting for pro-life doctors and nurses. On September 11, a groundbreaking ceremony was held at the location of the planned Holy Innocents center, signaling commencement of work on the derelict site purchased for the purpose. Less than a week shy of his seventieth birthday, the ghetto priest was as indomitable as ever in his undaunted work for the poor. He was also still finding time to write full-scale operatic works, the latest of which, the semi-autobiographical *Jam Reggae Opera*, had its premiere at the national arena in October.

In 2010 Father Ho Lung was one of a dozen priests selected by author John Pontifex as "heroic" witnesses to the Faith in the twenty-first century. Pontifex's book, *Heroic Priests*, published by the international charity, Aid to the Church in Need, listed the ghetto priest alongside priests from China, Pakistan, Russia and South America as exemplars of holy missionary priests in an age of anti-Christian persecution. In a newspaper interview to coincide with his seventy-first birthday he mentioned how humbled he felt to find himself listed amongst these heroic priests of our times. He spent his birthday supervising the continuing work at Holy Innocents center, the construction of which had been held up because of bureaucratic delays in receiving the necessary planning permission. When asked what he would like as a birthday gift he responded that he would like a gift of $8 million Jamaican ($100,000 in U.S. dollars), which was the balance needed for the completion of the building. As ever, he was proceeding in good faith and in apparent fecklessness, believing with Dickens' Mr. Micawber that something would turn up. "I figure that the Lord has anointed me to be a beggar," he explained, chuckling. "He said ask and you shall receive, knock and it shall be opened to you."[2]

*   *   *

The newspaper interview concluded with Father Ho Lung revealing "four things people would be surprised to know about you," his revelations echoing the answers that his good friend Wynton Williams had given when asked to reveal aspects of Father Ho Lung's private life two years earlier. Father Ho Lung revealed that he loved "run a boat" cooking, a traditional Jamaican way of preparing food thriftily by using anything one could afford or that came to hand. He particularly enjoyed making "a nice soup with a whole heap of things like goat head and callaloo, throwing in okra and anything." He liked nothing better, he explained, than cooking in a huge pot for 120 Brothers.

Sports were another favorite pastime: "I like sports. I play racquetball three times a week to keep fit. . . . I like football too but I can't keep up . . . I just watch." He added that the African Brothers invariably won the soccer games, trouncing the Indian and Filipino Brothers. He liked Jamaican music, particularly "reggae, mento, ska, dancehall and revival" and surprisingly listed as one of his favourite musicians the reggae artist Buju Banton, who at the time was remanded in custody in Miami on drugs charges and would later be convicted and sentenced to a ten-year federal prison sentence. "I still like a lot of Buju Banton's music. He has gotten in trouble now, but I still think he wrote some very nice music, and Bob Marley

2. *Sunday Observer*, September 26, 2010.

too." From one extreme to the other, Father Ho Lung listed the fourth thing that people might be surprised to know about him as being his love of gardening and the fact that he liked "being one with nature": "We have a little orchid house that the Brothers take care of; I love planting and seeing things grow. I love animals; we have sixty sheep, 150 pigs, 350 rabbits, we have cows and I love them and love taking care of them. We actually have a farm up in the mountain that helps us with meat and milk."

In 2011, as the MOP celebrated thirty years of service to the poor, Father Ho Lung could survey the achievement of the Brothers with a degree of satisfaction. In addition to the well established missions in Jamaica, India, the Philippines, Haiti, Uganda, and the United States, new missions had recently been established in Kenya and Indonesia. Also, and perhaps most important and gratifying of all, Holy Innocents, the center for mothers and babies, was finally opened on September 11 in the Kingston ghetto, exactly two years after the initial ground-breaking ceremony.

The other major development in the MOP in 2011 was the establishment of the Missionaries of the Poor Sisters. The first sisters had received their habits at the inaugural Mass at Holy Innocents center, a truly joyous occasion at which I was blessed to be present. In January 2012 I interviewed Sister Joanne Belmonte, one of the new Missionary Sisters, asking her how she first became involved. She told me that Father Ho Lung had approached her in 2007 about the plans for Holy Innocents center. At that time he was looking for lay women to help run the center because working with pregnant women did not seem appropriate work for the Brothers. In 2009 he began to think that perhaps a community of religious sisters was needed to run the center and asked Joanne to consider taking religious vows. "I thought I was too old to become a religious sister," she laughed, but she prayed on the matter and, inspired by the biblical figures of Sarah and Elizabeth, she felt that she was indeed called to become one of Father Ho Lung's pioneering new sisters. She was joined by Sister Melanie, who, like Sister Joanne, is a native of Toronto, by Sisters Emily and Claire, both from New York, and by Sister Ashley and Sister Chartalle, Jamaicans from near Kingston.

> When I interviewed Sister Joanne she was excited by the new ultrasound machines that had just been donated to the MOP. "We are going to be offering a clinic once a week for any woman who wants an ultrasound because it's very expensive to have an ultrasound here in Jamaica. We want them to hear the heartbeat. For those women who are considering an abortion the ultrasound machine is the ultimate weapon. It's a weapon against the abortion because when they hear the heartbeat and when the mother hears or sees the baby and sees a little hand, or sees the foot kicking or the baby sucking its thumb, it's far less likely that they will want to abort their child. We give the mothers a picture of their baby to take home. The ultrasound is a weapon against abortion, a weapon against the destruction of a human life."

I was present on the day that the ultrasounds were first used at the clinic and saw the excitement on Father Ho Lung's face as he watched the Sisters using this new weapon in the MOP's pro-life armory. "The whole 'pro-life' issue summarizes what the Brothers have been doing all along," he told me, "but we didn't know that it would all come together in this way. Saving babies is pivotal in the war between God and Satan. I began to understand that Satan really hates people. He hates people. He hates life. He has absolutely total repugnance for all that God has created and the destruction of the world is what he is all about. And I began to really see that the Lord is the giver of life. He is the source of life and, in terms of the Missionaries of the Poor, I can see that the life and the work of the Brothers has always been animated by the love of life and the protection of life."

It was singularly and symbolically appropriate that Holy Innocents, a center dedicated to the protection and preservation of human life, should be opened on the tenth anniversary of the September 11 terrorist attacks. It was an affirmation of the Resurrection, the triumph of life over the culture of death. In an age in which Herod is the hero and in which the slaughter of babies is promoted, Father Ho Lung had emerged as a lover and protector of the holy innocents.

Chapter Twenty-Four

....

THE JOY OF SUFFERING

Servitium Dulce cum Cristo Crucifixo.
(Joyful Service with Christ on the Cross.)
Motto of the Missionaries of the Poor

WHILE 2011 marked the thirtieth anniversary of the Missionaries of the Poor, it also marked the fortieth anniversary of Father Ho Lung and Friends. The anniversary was celebrated in style in early October with the staging at the national arena in Kingston of *Acts of the Apostles*, described on the cover of the official program as "an Opera . . . Epic . . . Gigantic . . . Magnificent!" As one among the many thousands of people who attended the show, I can confirm that such a description is not merely hyperbolic. *Acts of the Apostles* is certainly an epic of gigantic proportions, and as an opera it is certainly magnificent. In particular, the presentation of the beatific vision at the opera's climax is positively Wagnerian!

In an interview with Father Ho Lung and music director Wynton Williams on the morning after I'd seen the show, I commented that the climax was astonishing considering that the performance was basically low-tech, with no light shows or high-tech electronics. Father Ho Lung agreed: "The local singers, I might also add, are all volunteers, but they have extraordinary talent."

I wondered how the music was integrated into the wider mission of the MOP. To what extent was it part of the fabric of the lives of the Brothers? Was it simply a way of raising money for the centers and the missions? Does it help the community itself? Do the Brothers pull together in a different or special way that wouldn't be the case otherwise? Does it allow the MOP to integrate more effectively with the local community in Jamaica?

"Often times the music becomes a herald, like a trumpet blast, for the works of the brothers," said Williams. "The two support each other. The concerts are evangelical. They really get the message out, and the spirit of real elation and joy. There is catharsis. You feel that people are being moved by the witness of these young men, and the singers become part of the whole process of integrating with the brothers, and sharing in the effort to just lift up a message of bliss."

I was also intrigued by the way that the music of Father Ho Lung and Friends, which is composed by Father Ho Lung and arranged by Wynton Williams, had transitioned over the years from being very ethnically Jamaican towards a style that is almost classically operatic. Had this transition had an impact, negatively or positively, on the reception of the musicals by the general public in Kingston? Obviously, one would imagine that reggae is much more accessible than opera. "You know, I think it's changing," said Williams. "I think people, when they come to our shows, come with open hearts and minds. I get that impression, and by the fact that the audience continues to come in large numbers. As for the musical forms, we try to blend in many different genres of music. The operatic doesn't seem to be a distraction because it's not hard-core European *per se* but is mellowed somewhat with what could be seen as contemporary pop."

I suggested that the overall effect was reminiscent of Andrew Lloyd Webber, a suggestion which seemed to please Williams, who confessed that he had been "somewhat influenced by his style." Father Ho Lung added that the musical form was also connected to the themes being portrayed. "We let the music emerge naturally, but when you're depicting hell and heaven, those huge, huge themes, you have to allow your imagination to be true to the reality that you are trying to express." So, I interjected whimsically, Wagner is more appropriate than Desmond Dekker for a depiction of heaven or hell. "Right!" Father Ho Lung laughed. "Again, it comes down to being true to yourself. You want to be a little bit polemical in a way, but really, you really want to be true to yourself. You want to be true to what is there. I can't pretend that I'm not influenced by European music, or by American pop, because that's part of my background. And Jamaica is awfully close to the United States. It's not consistency in style that is most important, but the authenticity of the point of view. Whatever you are doing, it must come freely, and that's where the Holy Spirit is really leading you."

Considering the transition to the more operatic style, Father Ho Lung admitted to being shocked that people from the ghetto would come to see the shows three or four times. Wynton Williams agreed: "These are hard-core, steeped-in-the-ghetto-culture people, but they come back."

"They are opening up culturally," added Father Ho Lung. "They're opening culturally, which is really what you want. You don't want to get entrenched in a limited perspective. And, to our surprise, kids who are really tough, hip-hop types come, and they come in their thousands and thousands. And then they come back again a second time. They bring their moms and dads. And they listen, and they listen very carefully.

I don't think they assimilate everything but they allow the art to be itself."

I suggested that great art should stretch us. It should enable us to grow. We should feel that it is moving on a crystal floor over our heads, eluding the fullness of our grasp, beyond our reach but lifting us up. This is true of sanctity but also of culture. Some people are holier than we are and others are much better read than we are, or, in terms of music, much more musical and better versed in different types of music. We're not necessarily meant to understand everything when we read what these people have written or listen to what they have composed, but they're stretching us. We don't get it all, but it's leading us on. "That's correct," said Wynton. "That's right."

"We know there is something larger than us at work," said Father Ho Lung. "It's really marvelous. You saw it at the arena. You can have the richest person, you can have the most political of persons in the audience, and then you have the ghetto people, and you have the kids, and it's just wonderful because you feel that this is nation-building in the name of Christ, which is exactly our purpose, to engage people on a level who would not otherwise be engaged. And our Archbishop called and told me that he had come to the show and thought it was amazing. He said that through the musical and through the works of the brothers, people are being engaged in the Church who would otherwise be totally unreachable."

*   *   *

In November 2011, Father Ho Lung flew to the Philippines to receive the Gusi Peace Prize, the Third World's equivalent of the Nobel Peace Prize, a great honor. Initially, however, he was somewhat "ambivalent" about receiving the award and asked whether he could send Brother Ambrose to receive it on his behalf. On being told that he would have to travel to Manila to receive the award in person, he decided to make a virtue of necessity by arranging other activities while he was there. "I realized that it would generate a lot of interest for the missions, particularly in the East. I decided to travel to receive the award, but for no other reason really than to spread the word, to evangelize." Brother Charles, an Indian Brother, went ahead to prepare a number of other activities to make the trip worthwhile. "Frankly, the award doesn't mean very much to me but Brother Charles organized a dinner in Manila at which I was able to really talk to the Filipino people about the MOP missions in the Philippines." In his speech, which received widespread media coverage, Father Ho Lung warned of the perils of following the destructive contraceptive culture of the West, which would lead, he said, to the legalization of abortion. After receiving the award, he visited the brothers at Naga City, the main MOP mission in the Philippines, where, at another fundraising dinner, he spoke of the importance of the Church and urged church leaders in the Philippines to fight fearlessly in the battle for life against the forces of the culture of death. Finally, Father Ho Lung visited the MOP's mission in Cebu where he presided at a groundbreaking ceremony for a new home for the elderly. Continuing the pro-life theme that animated the visit, Father Ho Lung's speech focused on the importance of the Philippines as a very precious country because of its devout Catholicism and that Filipinos "needed to be aware of the enemy and not be tempted by European or US aid to accept abortion and the contraceptive culture."

As for the Gusi Award ceremony itself, Father Ho Lung felt ill at ease amongst the illustrissimi of opulent secularism. He attempted to fathom the philosophy behind the award and wondered what the organizers were trying to achieve. As an introduction to the secular vision for renewing the face of the earth in accordance with "the trends of our times" it was illuminating but ultimately fatuous. "From that point of view I was disappointed. There was a huge crowd, which didn't bother me too much, but I kept asking what was the purpose of it all? Where was it all leading and why were we here? Is the Gusi Award simply about being famous and great and so forth? It didn't make much sense to me anyway. It lacked any kind of incisiveness about its final purpose. Ultimately I resigned myself to its contradictions and emptiness. I said, okay, it is what it is." He also consoled himself with the knowledge that he was at least representing the Church and the Church's position in an environment in which they would otherwise be absent.

The grotesque irony was that Father Ho Lung was being awarded a "peace" prize by those who lacked any real concept of peace. Theirs was not the peace that passeth all understanding but the "peace" that lacketh any understanding. As Father Ho Lung's life and work illustrates, peace is not an abstract principle but a concrete reality. Indeed—joy of joys—peace is a Person. "When we meet the poor and we meet Christ in the poor," says Father Ho Lung, "there is something in you and there is something in the poor that comes alive. Like a seed that is planted in the ground, it comes alive and you're delighted. What is this thing in me? What is this thing in me that is now so alive? My faith is alive. I am alive. I see things from a different perspective. It's beyond words because it's really very mysterious." This is true peace. This is the peace that Father Ho Lung has in abundance and which he wishes to share with everyone he meets.

It is easy enough to mouth pious platitudes about the poor, to talk about Psalm 72 or the beatitudes, but this is only living the Gospel in the abstract. At some point, the life of a Christian can't just be abstract, it has to be incarnate. It needs to become a concrete reality. The poor are the concrete reality by which our faith becomes incarnate. When visitors to the MOP centers find themselves face to face with the poorest of the poor, with the least lovable, with the untouchables, they also find themselves face to face with the crucified Jesus in a truly radical and life-changing sense. "We need to be like Thomas," says Father Ho Lung. "We need to put our hands in the wounds of the crucified Christ on earth. It is then that we believe. It is then that we come alive. So many visitors have come to us over the years and they work all day long and they come back full of joy."

Peace is the Real Presence of Christ, says Father Ho Lung. "Through His works He is present in the word. If you discover Him in the word, that is great. He is also present in the Eucharist, and in all of the sacraments, but in a very special way in the Eucharist. And He is also really present in the poor and in you and me."

The lesson that I've learned from my own experience of working at the centers is that when you see and touch and meet the poor, you are receiving a gift. What you're doing for them is nothing compared with the gift that you are receiving from them. I realized for the first time the full truth of Christ's promise that his yoke is easy and his burden is light. Indeed I realized that his burden was light not merely in the sense that it was not burdensome but in the sense that it was the light in the darkness of our lives, the light by which we see. "The light of your eyes is Jesus," says Father Ho Lung in the lyrics of one of his songs. The Cross of Christ is the light by which we see. Without the Cross, without suffering, we are blind. The MOP centers, then, are places where the blind learn to see. They are often infirmaries for the poor, but they also serve as hospitals where the wealthy receive riches from the poor and where the healthy are healed by the sick.

If the modern world needs to learn the paradox that Peace is to be found in the Cross, or, more correctly, *on* the Cross, it also needs to understand that Love is also to be found hanging from the Cross and that it cannot be found anywhere else. It was a truth unknown to John Lennon that "all you need is love" is synonymous with "all you need is Christ."

"Learning to love is very important," says Father Ho Lung. "But learning to love in a way that leads to self-sacrifice, redefines love, I think, for the modern world, where 'love' is so carnal and self-indulgent, and where, very often, love is really selfishness, the very reverse of what it is meant to be." Love can be defined as a self-sacrificial giving of oneself to the Other. In this sense Christ's giving of himself to and for humanity on the Cross is the archetype of all love and Christ himself is the archetype of all lovers. All true love is but a copy or type of this Love and all true lovers but copies or types of this one Lover. "The spirituality of the brothers is to love and to teach others how to love," Father Ho Lung explains, indicating that the Brothers are called to imitate Christ. "It has been apparent to me that God's will for our community is to love, to learn how to love and to teach others how to love by our example."

Considering that peace and love reside with Christ on the Cross, it is no surprise that the motto of the Missionaries of the Poor is "Joyful Service with Christ on the Cross." Note that the motto does not say joyful service *of* Christ on the Cross, but joyful service *with* him on the Cross. Joy is not to be found in quiet contemplation of the crucified Christ if such contemplation means that we are simply at the foot of the Cross staring up at Him. We cannot be merely spectators of Christ's Passion. We must seek to die with him. A sword must pierce our souls also. Father Brian, one of the MOP's founding members, emphasizes that the motto of the MOP "really does bring out some fundamental and key principles of the MOP's spirituality in its stress on Christ, and not just the Christ that is Risen but the wounded Christ, reminding us that the heart of love and life is sacrifice." Moving from the sacrificial heart of the paradox of love and life, Father Brian then proceeded to the joy to be discovered in the depths of that sacrificial heart: "The most beautiful thing that Father Ho Lung teaches is that the life of suffering and sacrifice is an invitation to happiness. The call to serve the poor is an invitation to happiness. Father Ho Lung keeps saying that he's the happiest man on the face of the earth. Despite all the crosses he sees around him, he claims he's the happiest man on the earth."

We began this celebration of Father Ho Lung and the Missionaries of the Poor with an affirmation that the acceptance of suffering was the secret of life and that when we understood that we would understand everything. We end, however, by discovering that the mere acceptance of suffering is not enough. We need to embrace suffering. We need to desire it as the means by which the fruits of peace, love, joy and happiness are to be attained. We need to offer our hands, feet and heart to the nails of humanity's suffering and to the lance of Divinity's Love in order to reach the place that Love Himself has prepared for us in His own offering of hands, feet and heart for our sake. In our joyful service with Christ on the Cross we can become, like Father Ho Lung, the happiest men on earth in the knowledge that we are destined to be happier still in Heaven.

INDEX

THE MISSIONARIES OF THE POOR (MOP) take vows of poverty, chastity, obedience and free service to the poorest of the poor.

Father Ho Lung and the MOP priests and brothers surrender all rights to their own material possessions, bodily desires, will and remuneration for services rendered to the poor. They have no private possessions and no bank accounts. The MOP live in community, sharing all things in common.

The material needs of the MOP are supplied by the generosity of readers like you—readers who share their faith, embrace their mission and offer their own resources to serve the poor.

To learn how you can assist the MOP in their mission and join them in serving the poor, visit their website at www.missionariesofthepoor.org.

Or contact them at:

Missionaries of the Poor
3 North Street
Kingston, Jamaica, WI
(876) 948-0280 or
(876) 948-6173
mopja@missionariesofthepoor.org